C0-AMY-515

THE RISE AND FALL
OF THE
NEW ROMAN EMPIRE

By the same author

STRUGGLE FOR A CONTINENT

The Rise and Fall of the New Roman Empire

Italy's bid for World Power, 1890-1943

GLEN ST. J. BARCLAY

'Arm the prow, and sail into the world'
D'ANNUNZIO, *La Nave*

St. Martin's Press
New York

St. Martin's Press, Inc., 175 Fifth Avenue,
New York, N.Y. 10010
Library of Congress Catalog Card Number: 72-97412
First published in the United States of America in 1973

AFFILIATED PUBLISHERS: Macmillan & Company, Limited, London — also at Bombay, Calcutta, Madras and Melbourne.

Printed in Great Britain

Contents

List of Illustrations

Acknowledgements

I should wish to express my appreciation of the unfailing friendliness and assistance provided by the Director and staff of the Italian Institute, Belgrave Square, London, where much of the research for this book was completed.

Preface

It has become a truism to say that Italy is the enigma of Europe. Italian military and diplomatic leadership after the First World War was as difficult for contemporary Europeans to understand as Italian economic leadership after the Second. But bewilderment at Italian achievement can be overdone. The fact is that Italy has provided a more consistently dynamic element in the development of Europe over the past eighty years than any other nation. The last and least of the emergent European Great Powers was also the first to develop a truly modern navy; the first to defeat the Dervishes in Africa; the first to use aircraft as weapons of war; the one which fought the greatest of colonial wars, which perfected the first Blitzkriegs, which dominated the Continent in aviation and automotive technology for over ten years. It was also, more significantly, the Power whose assaults on the Turkish Empire produced the conditions out of which the First World War arose; whose intervention on the Entente side made possible the victory of the Entente, to which it contributed proportionately more than any other belligerent; whose power and authority in the late 1930s could have guaranteed the maintenance of peace in Europe, and averted the ultimate calamity of the Second World War, but for the readiness of the British and French to abandon Italy and the Mediterranean bloc to Hitler, as they were ready to abandon Czechoslovakia; as they were ready to abandon Russia.

The enduring importance of Italy as a factor in the European system is of course still obscured by the extent of Italian military failure in the Second World War, exaggerated as it was at the time by Allied propaganda, because of the need to insist that at least one of the Powers against which the British Empire was fighting was even less prepared for modern war than Britain itself was, despite the fact that Italian aviators and seamen, most conspicuously in the MAS flotillas, frequently carried their service to the utmost limits of human courage and dedication. It is indeed salutary to recall now how close the Italians came in 1942 to winning the war for themselves and their German partners. One more British merchantman sunk in the Battle of mid-August would have meant the fall of Malta; the fall of Malta would have meant total Axis victory in North Africa; and total Axis victory in North Africa would have meant that an Anglo-American invasion force would have had to be hurled directly against Western Europe, without the assistance of diversionary moves against Algeria or Italy itself, in the face of defending forces probably twice as strong as those available to the Axis in 1944.

The purpose of this study is simply to describe the nature of Italian influence in Europe, and by extension in Africa, during the half century between 1890 and 1943; the means by which it was exerted; and the consequences of Italian success or failure for the other nations involved. It might be suggested that such an examination is particularly appropriate at a time when Italian economic development is setting the pace for the European Economic Community, the nature of which is about to be changed significantly by the entry of the United Kingdom – engineered largely by Italian diplomacy – in the interests of the oldest of Italian foreign policy objectives, the preservation of the Balance of Power in Europe. It is time to consider Italy again.

1 : Return to Africa

STANLEY met Livingstone at Ujiji in Tanganyika on 11 November 1871. The Parliament of the newly united Kingdom of Italy met in Rome for the first time seventeen days later. There was, of course, no connection between the two events. But Italians, at once euphoric and apprehensive over their decisive step to nationhood,[1] were ready to find a symbolic one. The coincidence of dates recalled their historic links with the continent across the Mediterranean, and pointed the direction in which their destiny might yet lie. There was indeed nowhere else for them to go, for the time being. The new Kingdom had the misfortune to be surrounded on three sides by vast and forbidding Great Powers. France lay, truculent and disapproving, to the west; the Austro-Hungarian Empire loomed ominously to the north; and any adventures eastwards, into the Balkans, were liable to add the fury of Britain to that of the other Empires involved. Africa offered the only prospects of glory and economic profit. There were also obvious historical associations: Roman rule had been effective along some part at least of the entire coastline of North Africa, for nearly five hundred years, and this connection had not been utterly lost since the days of Augustus. Merchants from Genoa, Florence and Naples had constantly maintained trading links with the African kingdoms. The Italian explorers Finati and Minutoli had been among the first Europeans to enter the Sudan between 1815 and 1820, although these expeditions were not wholly Italian. And there had even been a clash of arms. Italian sea power had made its potency felt in North Africa on 25 September 1825, when Chevalier Sori led a squadron of five Piedmontese ships into the harbour of Tripoli to remind the Bey of his obligations to foreign commerce. The usual Turkish response of rhodomontade and abuse had been met with a seaborne assault that destroyed three Egyptian ships and an arsenal, and brought the Bey to terms within twenty-four hours,[2] thus achieving more striking results in considerably less time than the Americans had done thirteen years before.

But the Italians had reasons for considering a return to Africa more pressing than historical relationships, a certain need for a dramatic foreign policy, and a nostalgic flicker of naval glory. Poverty and political oppression had helped to ensure that there were far more people in the Peninsula in the middle of the nineteenth century whom the authorities wished to lock up than there were gaol cells to put them in. Sicilian and Piedmontese governments had been looking for suitable penal colonies ever since the 1820s. North Africa itself was, regrettably, unpromising for developments of this kind, Morocco being too inaccessible; Algeria having already been invaded by the French in 1830; Tunis, Tripoli and Cyrenaica being provinces of the Turkish Empire, whose integrity was cherished by the British ever since it had become their major continental trading partner;[3] and Egypt under Mehemet Ali having become a Great Power in its own sphere, independent and expansionist to the extent that it had threatened to overrun the Turkish Empire itself in 1827. The problem was to find a suitably weak and accessible African state, lacking powerful foreign protectors. Abyssinia seemed to be the obvious answer.

Political and economic relations between that obscure state and the European Powers had effectively begun in 1809, when the British had opened negotiations with Ras Welde Selassie, to establish regular trade between Abyssinia and the East India Company.[4] In 1840 the British and French had opened competing consulates in Abyssinia at Massawa, on the Red Sea, which were followed by further commercial treaties between Britain and the dissident local rulers of the Abyssinian hinterland between 1841 and 1849,[5] placing Abyssinia clearly in Europe's sphere of consciousness. Italian interest was further whetted in 1855, when Andre de Bono succeeded in navigating the White Nile, near the ill-defined, south-western frontier of Abyssinia. By 1857 Cavour was seriously meditating plans for a united Italy to establish its colonial empire on the base of a crumbling and impotent East African anachronism.[6]

Abyssinia was about to be made much more accessible to European contacts. Ferdinand de Lesseps had obtained permission from the Khedive in 1854 to form a company to construct a canal through the Isthmus of Suez and work was actually begun in 1858. But the opportunity for easy colonization of East Africa had already been lost: the anachronism was no longer crumbling. In 1852 the second most charismatic and spectacular of Abyssinian rulers had set out on his own programme of unification and aggrandizement. Kedaref Kassa broke the power of the old feudal princes in three years; seized the imperial throne of Gondar, under the title of Tewodoros (Theodore) II; and began encouraging approaches from the Europeans, in the hope of enlisting their support for an Abyssinian invasion of Egypt, where Mehemet's successors were completing their own plans to carve out a great Egyptian Empire in the Sudan and East Africa, precisely where Tewodoros was plotting his own incursion against themselves. This imbroglio of conflicting and rapacious African imperialists might well have seemed an excellent occasion for raids and intrigues by the Europeans against a continent at war with itself. And the Kingdom of Italy in 1866 seemed as well equipped as any for this kind of colonial enterprise. It was, admittedly, still the least populous of the Great Powers: Italy's population of twenty-six millions ranked behind Britain's twenty-eight millions, France's thirty-eight, Germany's thirty-nine and Russia's seventy-three; but the Italians were consistently maintaining the highest rate of natural increase in Europe. And their capacity for maritime expansion seemed to be very much greater than their numbers or material strength might have indicated.

The enormous expension of their merchant marines during the Crimean War, and the loss by sale or destruction of nearly three-quarters of the shipping of the United States during the Civil War, had combined to raise Italy to the position of being, in effect, the third maritime Power in the world. And this eminence was not confined to commercial shipping. The Italian fleet in 1865 was, on paper, the most impressive naval striking force of any nation; containing some of the newest, fastest, best-armed and most heavily armoured fighting ships in the world.[7] All that it lacked so far was an opportunity to show in battle that its admirals knew how to deploy the deadly weapons under their command. If they did, then Italy could embark upon a policy of colonial adventurism on the high seas as confidently as ever the Spanish, British, Dutch and French had done in the past.

That opportunity came in 1866. Bismarck's decision to force Austria out of German affairs gave the Italians the perfect occasion to show the world that a great new military and naval power had arrived. Plans were prepared with the Prussians during the spring for joint action, and then on 20 July Italy enthusiastically went to war with the Austrian Empire, to liberate the Peninsula 'from the Alps to the Adriatic'. The task seemed easy – a field army of 263,000 was available for immediate action. The Austrians on the other hand could spare barely 135,000 to defend their southern provinces, at least 70,000 of the men were committed to garrison duties, which left only 65,000 at most free to be deployed in battle.

But the Italians had their problems too. Their original plan had indeed been to hurl a bold thrust to the heart of the Austrian Empire, but this had been vetoed by Napoleon III of France, who had no wish to see Austria weakened so badly that it would no longer be able to operate as a counterbalance to the power of Prussia in Western Europe. He had accordingly opened negotiations with the Austrians to secure Italian neutrality by conceding Venetia, while retaining the Tyrol and Trentino. The Italian Chief of Staff, General La Mamora, apparently found it difficult to see the purpose in fighting for territory which the Austrians were seemingly prepared to give up anyway, and he assumed that the Austrians would be sensible enough to see things in the same light. But leaders of Great Powers do not think along those lines, as the Italians, as aspirants to greatness, should have known. So La Mamora's great army, lacking any kind of offensive purpose, rambled eagerly across the frontier towards Verona, to find itself confronted with an Austrian army less than a third the size of its own, but occupying the high ground above the Adige River, with its position secured by some of the strongest fortifications in Europe, and with a commanding officer who knew exactly what he was there for, and who was determined to defeat the Italians again on the same place where, seven years previously, his predecessors had defeated them. And although La Mamora was prepared to go to war, he was not prepared to do any fighting – a position quite often adopted by Italian commanders. La Mamora, however, actually coped with the problem in quite a creditable manner. He organized 110,000 men from his disarrayed and wearied troops for an impromptu attack, while the other corps looked on in bewilderment, and tried to drive the Austrians from a position in which they enjoyed every advantage except numbers. A very slightly greater degree of determination could have given La Mamora the first Italian land victory in history. As it was, when he called off the assault, convinced of the impossibility and indeed the futility of breaking the splintering Austrian lines, his men had inflicted 5,000 casualties on the enemy, at a cost to themselves of 720 dead and 3,112 wounded. But the retreat soon redressed this balance. Another 4,000 Italians fell into the hands of the exhausted Austrians as prisoners, while La Mamora fell back to regroup against a counter-attack that his opponent could never have delivered. La Mamora had snatched defeat from the jaws of victory, and he never got an opportunity to redeem himself. The reinforcements, rushed by Austria to the Italian front were recalled as hastily for the defence of Vienna after Sadowa. The south lay open and undefended, so that La Mamora's liberators were met only by welcoming civilians when he led them tentatively into Venetia again.

In managing this war, La Mamora had shown admirable humanitarian qualities, but, unfortunately, one does not go to war in the first place for humanitarian considerations. The Italians had not even gone to war primarily to regain territory: they had gone to strengthen national unity and to serve notice to the world that they were henceforth to be treated with the respect befitting a Great Power. And as the army had strikingly failed to convey this impression, it was now up to the strongest fleet in Europe to do better. King Victor Emmanuel had indeed ordered Admiral Persano some twelve days before the outbreak of war to be ready to 'sweep the enemy from the Adriatic and to attack and blockade them wherever he should find them', orders which should have been well within his power to carry out. He commanded in all some twenty-six ships with 641 guns, including twelve ironclads, whereas the Austrian Admiral von Tegetthoff had only seven ironclads among his twenty-one ships, all of them older and more lightly armoured than the Italian ones, and mounting in all only 532 guns, throwing about half the weight of the Italians' broadside.

Naval authorities throughout the world had been awaiting the outcome of what should have been one of the most significant engagements in naval history. Armour, steam propulsion and rifled cannon had all previously been used at sea, in the American Civil War, but they had been employed in what were essentially artillery duels on water, between almost stationary monitors. This would be the first time since the introduction of gunpowder that great fleets had manoeuvred on the high seas, using against each other the apparatus of a completely new technology. Navies of the modern age were to do battle for the first time in the Adriatic.

The sense of occasion was too much for Persano. Six weeks after receiving his orders to wage an aggressive sea war, he was still putting his sailors (who were admittedly inexperienced) through practice drills, in a place far removed from any risk of a chance encounter with the Austrians. But his attempts to save his new ships and his own reputation from the hazards of combat were brought to failure by peremptory orders from King Victor Emmanuel himself. The King ordered the fleet summarily to 'attempt whatever actions may be thought likely to obtain a success'. There was not much time: the Austrians were likely to sue for peace at any moment. Persano duly decided to attack the nearest Austrian position he could reach, which happened to be the island of Lissa (Vis) off the coast of Yugoslavia. He was, however, attacked there himself by Tegetthoff on the morning of 20 July, while involved in the most critical phase of an amphibious operation, that of actually disembarking his landing parties. The ensuing battle did not make history: its only contribution to the art of war was to set back four hundred years the study of naval tactics. In spite of steam, armour and rifling, both navies used methods of attack discarded since the days of galleys. Admiral Tegetthoff simply ordered his armoured ships 'to rush upon and sink the enemy'. Persano rationally tried to counter this barbaric approach by using his superior gun power, but he then threw his already disordered formation into complete chaos by shifting his flag from one ship to another, giving himself freedom to manoeuvre out of the line of battle. The result was that the great Italian fleet floundered about in the fog and smoke while its Admiral tried industriously to ram the onrushing Austrians. After four hours of fighting, the Italians had 706 casualties whilst the Austrians had only 176; their newest and strongest armoured ship had been rammed and sunk by a wooden Austrian vessel; another armoured gunboat had been blown up by shell fire; and Persano's own flagship was crippled and sinking. The Austrians had not lost a ship. The strongest of sea powers had been defeated totally by the least maritime of empires.

Thus Custozza and Lissa failed to reinforce Italy's pretensions to be counted among the comity of Great Powers. They instead did everything to reinforce the idea already prevalent in Europe, that Italian interests need not be taken too seriously. This made it more urgent for Italy to embark on a successful programme of overseas expansion, especially if it could involve some easy military victories over ill-equipped native forces, which might restore the confidence of Italians in their own Kingdom, and also demonstrate that there were some peoples at least who had reason to fear Italian power. Practical arguments in favour of such action were more pressing than ever. For example, the prison system in Italy was in danger of collapse, with 44,000 Italians already incarcerated, and a further 10,000 on suspended sentences, waiting for prison accommodation. Moreover, the decision of the British to stop the deportation of felons to Australia in 1868 paradoxically reminded Europeans of the great benefits in trade and financial returns which, as the Australian experience suggested, could be derived from an intelligent use of the penal colony system in a favourable overseas environment. Spain, Denmark, Belgium and Portugal, as well as Italy, all began looking for their future Australias. And in the meantime the gate to Abyssinia swung open. Tewodoros' plans for conquest in the Sudan led him to arrest the British Consul in Massawa, as well as assorted missionaries, with the intention of forcing the British to open negotiations with him, and provide support for his projected invasions. What he received instead was a British invasion from India. In 1868, 11,770 British troops stormed his fortress at Magdala, killing 500 Abyssinians and with only thirty British wounded; and the House of Commons 'received with lively satisfaction' the news that the Emperor of Abyssinia had shot himself in despair, over the ruination of his plans for conquest.[8] Moreover, the humiliation of Abyssinian power at the hands of a European army was followed in 1869 by the opening of the Suez Canal for traffic, making the Red Sea enormously more accessible to European invaders. The Italian Government hoped to see a new Australia in Abyssinia. They accordingly induced the missionary, Father Guiseppe Sapeto, to act as an agent for the Societa di Navigazione Rabbatino, to acquire seven square miles of land around Assab, on the African side of the Straits of Mendeb, at the mouth of the Gulf of Aden. On 13 March 1870 the red-white-and-green Italian tricolour was raised over a factory at nearby Alala. They barely got there in time. A French expedition was already assembling at Toulon, aimed at nothing less than the conquest and annexation of the whole state of Abyssinia. But the French never sailed. The outbreak of the Franco-Prussian War on 19 July 1870 called a halt to French overseas adventures. The precarious Italian toehold at Assab was secure. The Romans were back in Africa.

They were not, however, back in Rome yet. But German victories in the West soon made it possible to rectify that omission. Italian troops occupied the ancient capital on 20 September, taking advantage of the recall of the French garrison to meet the threat to Paris. But this symbolic triumph, far from assisting the diplomatic and social problems of the Kingdom of Italy, actually exacerbated them. The fact that the Italians had been able to take advantage of French preoccupations to develop a factory at Assab and to seize Rome merely made it more evident that they would not have been able to do either had the French been free to stop them. Italy would have to do something on its own before it could be taken seriously as a Power of any standing. And Rome itself, instead of being a practical asset, was just another burden on the overstrained and inefficient public services of the Peninsula. It could hardly be said that Italy suffered from problems of overcrowding in the modern sense, but it did support a population two-thirds the size of the French on less than half that country's area; its national income per head was lower than that of any major Power except Russia; and its division into a congeries of petty states, generally mismanaged by incompetent and repressive autocrats, guaranteed that its economic organization and public utilities were among the least efficient in Europe. Unification had only intensified existing disparities and dislocation: the removal of frontier divisions meant that both capital and labour could move unhindered to the already prosperous north, increasing the strain on housing and public facilities there, and leaving the south with an increasing burden of poverty, and declining resources with which to alleviate it. In these circumstances, it is not surprising that the Italians should have thought that they had a population problem, and that it was getting worse. The flow of emigration was becoming a haemorrhage: 550,000 Italians were already living overseas, 11,000 of them in Tunis, just across the Mediterranean, but already within the shadow of French domination; and 330,000 had left in the past ten years. The government accordingly cast around for suitable overseas territories in which its people could be settled, either voluntarily as pioneers or involuntarily as deported felons, so that the fruits of their energies in either case would not be lost to the *patria*.

Italy was not the last of the great colonial Powers, as is often asserted.[9] Germany, Belgium, the United States and Japan had not really entered the race yet; the Spanish were still dreaming of regaining an empire in the Americas, and had not yet begun to acquire a new one in Africa; and only the British, the French and the Portuguese had established themselves to any significant degree upon the southern continent. But there was no doubt that Italy in 1870 was the least of the colonial Powers. And Assab was clearly not the answer. Seven square miles of sunbaked rock on the shores of the Red Sea were not going to solve anybody's population problem.

Negotiations were immediately opened in a world-wide search for prospective penal colonies, 'from the Aleutians to the Falklands';[10] with Denmark, for the Nicobar Islands in the Bay of Bengal; with the United Kingdom, for Socotra, in the Arabian Sea; and with Sweden, for San Barthelemy, in the West Indies. However, it was still Abyssinia which seemed to hold the greatest promise for exploitation. The only danger appeared to be that others might snatch the ripe plum first. The Khedive Ismail of Egypt was now embarked on a project to extend Egyptian economic domination over the whole of East Africa from the Sudan to Zanzibar; to ensure that the entire ivory trade would be diverted north to Cairo.[11] His lunge for the Indian Ocean was temporarily arrested when the British intervened at the plea of their vassal the Sultan of Zanzibar, and demanded the recall of an Egyptian invasion heading for Kismayu. Ismail then turned directly eastwards. Massawa and Suakin on the Red Sea fell under Egyptian control in 1865; a protectorate was established over Zeila, on the Gulf of Aden, in 1875; and in the following year assaults were commenced from the north and west against Abyssinia, which was already weakened by civil strife after the suicide of Tewodoros. East Africa was wide open for conquest.

It so happened that just then there was another Italian explorer-adventurer on the spot. Having circumnavigated Lake Albert in the Congo, Romolo Gessi, with orders from Gordon to organize a military campaign against young Sulieman's Arab slavers, had already approached the borderlands of Abyssinia. In 1878 he succeeded brilliantly, crushing Sulieman's forces at Bahr-el-Ghazal, and freeing 10,000 Negro slaves.[12] This achievement gave moral zeal to the colonialist enthusiasm building up in Italy. Gessi was hailed as the 'Garibaldi of Africa'; Cesare Correnti founded the Italian Geographical Society, and presented a huge exhibition aimed at proving that Italy was destined to become a great geographical Power; and the merchant-adventurer Pellegrino Mattieu urged that closer relations should be developed between Italy and Abyssinia, on the grounds that only Abyssinia among all the nations of the world could compare with Rome in terms of greatness and antiquity.[13]

Remarkably enough, the Abyssinians themselves had already made tentative approaches to their future conquerors. Young King Menelik of Shoa, naturally concerned at the Egyptian threat to his own designs on the imperial crown of his titular Lord, Yohannes IV, had written to King Victor Emmanuel, respectfully seeking advice and friendship. In March 1876 Orazio Antenori led an expedition to the court of Menelik, thereby, in effect, opening formal relations between Rome and Shoa, and it was the enthusiastic Mattieu who strengthened these links by heading a trade delegation to Menelik two years later. But the time for friendly and circumspect cultivation of Africa was already past. The strong were calling the tune, and again Italy had to pay the price of weakness.

For there was still one significant difference between the Rome of the past and the new Kingdom of Italy: whereas Rome's greatness had rested upon military invincibility, Italy had not yet demonstrated the capacity to deter any challenger. The demoralizing record of humiliation continued. Attempts to acquire penal colonies in the American hemisphere had to be terminated when the United States invoked a specious interpretation of the Monroe Doctrine, protesting against the transfer of territory within the hemisphere from one European Empire to another. This setback was followed by Italy's first independent venture into the arena of international arbitration, in a manner which brought nothing but disgrace upon the nation and its leaders. Russia and Austria had gradually been encroaching upon the crumbling frontiers of the Turkish Empire since the tide of Ottoman expansion westward was turned back at Vienna in the seventeenth century.

The Russian advance had been checked for a generation by defeat at the hands of the British, French and Piedmontese in the Crimea. Then in 1876 dissension in the Balkans paved the way for a new Russian sortie. But this in its turn was certain to lead to corresponding action by the Austrians, anxious to ensure that no Russian advance towards the Dardanelles should cut across their own predetermined line of progress towards Salonika. However, Austrian expansion along the coast of the Adriatic would open Italy's vulnerable coastline to assault from the east, as it was already exposed to French attacks from the west. It would also close off Italian access to the only area of the European continent where Rome might still hope to acquire an important influence.

In the situation that was developing there was nothing that the Italians could do on their own account to safeguard their interests. They could not stop the Russians, and they could not fight the Austrians. But it was conceivably open for them to do a deal with Vienna. In Italy more and more people were demanding the recovery of the northern provinces which had been taken by Austria in 1866. Garibaldi had appealed to all Italians still under Austrian rule to hold themselves ready for action against the Oppressor. It was at least imaginable that

Vienna might be prepared to yield the Trentino in return for Italian agreement to, or at least acceptance of, a further Austrian thrust into the Balkans. The matter called for the kind of delicate negotiation for which Italians were supposed to have a natural finesse. But Prime Minister Agostino Depretis thoroughly bungled the affair. He tactlessly sent a warning to Vienna that any further aggrandizement on Austria's part would alter the Balance of Power in Europe. And there was nothing that the Austrians were likely to heed less than a peremptory warning from Rome. Austrian Foreign Minister Andrassy, secure in an arrangement with St Petersburg and an alliance with Berlin, replied brutally that Austria would not content itself with defending its imperial possessions, but would attack at the first sign of annexationist intentions on Italy's part.

There was nothing to be done in the face of such a threat but to back down. Italy watched powerlessly while the Russians began their advance on Constantinople, and the British rushed forces to the Eastern Mediterranean to protect their threatened imperial life-line to India. Depretis cast around desperately for friends as the clouds darkened over Europe, but he had little choice in them. An approach to the Russians would only alienate Britain, before whose sea power the Italian coast would be helplessly exposed; France was still resentful over the siezure of Rome, and determined to frustrate Italian colonial ambitions in Africa; and Austria was nothing less than the designated national enemy. Francesco Crispi, the President of the Chamber of Deputies, was accordingly sent to approach Prince Bismarck for a German alliance against the Austrian menace. But Germany was already committed to a military alliance with Austria. Bismarck, however, tried to improve the situation by suggesting that Crispi should advise Depretis to annex Tunis, by way of compensation. But Italy was in no position to risk the confrontation with France which Bismarck had hoped would result from such an act. However, it was equally impossible for an Italian government to abandon its 11,000 compatriots in Tunis by taking up a counter-suggestion from Paris to acknowledge dominant French interests in Tunis in return for a free hand in Tripoli.

The fact was that Crispi and Depretis were too frightened of possible consequences by this time to do anything. They even declined an obviously suspect proposal from Vienna that they should establish themselves across the Adriatic by annexing Albania. The inevitable result was that they got nothing. Italy looked on helplessly while Turkish power in the Balkans was broken; Russia was forced to retreat from Constantinople in the face of united opposition by the Great Powers and Austria moved its authority into the northern provinces of Bosnia and Hercegovina, thrust into the narrow sallyport of Novibazar, between Montenegro and Serbia, and prepared for a further lunge for the Aegean. Depretis frantically tried to avert a further humiliation by ordering the ever-ready Rubattinis to buy up the railroad from Goletta to Tunis, in a weak bid to forestall the impending French encroachment. But the weak have no luck. The French could afford to be brutal. On 12 March they unconditionally declared a protectorate over Tunis. The Italian community across the Mediterranean had been taken over by Paris.

This was of course just what the Germans wanted. Italy had deliberately refused to provoke France by direct action in Tunis in 1878, when invited to do so by Bismarck. The French had responded to this display of moderation three years later with a deliberately provocative action in calculated disregard of the interests of a lesser power. The occupation of Tunis was pure aggression. France did not have a community of nationals to be protected, as Italy had; it did not need Tunis as a future target for immigration, as Italy did; it had no interest in the territory except that of preserving peace on the border of Algeria, which could have been done as well by the Italians, if they had been allowed to establish themselves there.

No government in the world could have accepted such a provocation without making some response. There was no doubt that Italy had to do something. It had been threatened by

Austria, discounted by Britain, ignored by Russia and ridiculed by Germany. It was now being threatened by Egypt, whose invading forces were moving in on Italy's client sultanates, Raheita and Bailut. No aspirant Great Power ever had to endure fifteen more utterly discouraging years. There was only one course of action open to Rome, and it was little more gratifying. Being unable to confront any of the Great Powers on its own Italy would have to seek the protection of the only Great Power with an interest in extending it. Negotiations were opened with Germany immediately for some arrangement to link Italy with the Austro-German Alliance. The terms finally agreed upon were the most convincing demonstration possible of Italy's weakness. King Umberto of Italy, Kaiser Wilhelm of Germany and the Emperor Franz Josef of Austria agreed on 20 May 1882 that they would not enter into an engagement with a foreign Power directed against any one of their number; that Austria and Germany would help Italy with all their forces if that country were the victim of an unprovoked attack by France; and that Italy on its part would do the same for Germany in a similar situation. The Treaty was described as being of an 'essentially conservative and defensive nature'. However, it amounted to a major defeat for Italy, in that the major objective of traditional Italian foreign policy had been abandoned. Italy was admittedly not bound actually to go to the defence of its Austrian enemy, but it was debarred alike from joining with another power in an attack on Austria, or from taking advantage of a war of aggression by Austria against anybody else. The Trentino and the Tyrol had been abandoned to Austria in order to buy German protection against France.

There was only one consolation. Italy could now pursue its objectives in Africa, freed from the dangers of French rivalry. And indeed it was high time to resume colonial adventuring, if only to distract the minds of the Italian people from the implications of the Triple Alliance. Fortunately, the occasion had already presented itself. Africa was calling again. Ismail's invasion of Abyssinia had been turned back in 1877 by the Emperor

Yohannes, after a campaign in which more than 10,000 Egyptians had been killed. Abyssinia had preserved its integrity. But then in November 1881 Muhammad Ahmad assumed the title of Mahdi, or Saviour of Islam, in the Sudan,[14] and proclaimed a religious war against Turkish rule, meaning in this case the authority of Ismail, whose extravagances were already engendering mutiny and disaffection in Egypt itself. The British and French began to consider intervention, to protect their interests in the Suez Canal. The Italian government saw in this a double opportunity: they could take advantage of the distraction of the other interested powers to extend their own area of control in Africa; and they could ingratiate themselves with either of the two major colonial Powers, by offering their support to whichever was more disposed to accept it. They accordingly bought out the Rubattinis, assumed authority over Assab, and waited for developments, meantime reopening talks with Menelik of Shoa, through whose domains any line of Italian advance would have to proceed.

They did not have to wait long this time. On 26 April 1882 British Ambassador Paget and Italian Foreign Minister Mancini agreed that Italy was justified not only in developing its commercial and maritime interests in Assab, but also in constructing whatever military works were necessary in the area to safeguard those interests. In May the British and French bombarded Alexandria, deposed the embarrassing Ismail, and restored the Khedive Tewfik to power in Cairo. The British then considered reasserting Egyptian control in the Sudan by force, only to find themselves deserted by the French, who had failed to obtain from London the free hand they sought in west and central Africa. Italy was a superfluous power no longer. Paget proposed on 25 July that Italy should co-operate directly with Britain and France in the Egyptian imbroglio. Italian diplomacy was finally worthy of the occasion. After discussions with Germany and Austria, Mancini proposed instead that Italy should act as a member of a joint European police force to protect the Suez Canal, thus avoiding any prospect of the enterprise becoming too narrowly a British exercise of power; the British and French, mutually suspicious in any event, hastened to agree; and on 10 August 1882 the iron-clad *Affondatore* sailed to take its place in an international fleet to guard the waterway. Italy counted at last.

More than that, it was positively being sought after, as British problems multiplied in the Sudan. British Foreign Minister Lord Granville expressed his view on 8 October that 'considerable benefit may accrue to the tribes through the civilising influence of Italy . . .'. Britain would accordingly avoid anything that might 'throw difficulties in the way of the extension of Italian authority inland from Assab'.[15] Mancini for his part was sure that annexations by any Power other than Italy on the Red Sea littoral would 'not consist with British interests'; and he assumed that Britain 'would look without jealousy on a moderate extension of the colony of Assab . . . in whatever form it would be found convenient'.[16] But the British were paying a different game: whereas Rome was seeking involvement in Africa, London was seeking disengagement. Egyptian authority in the Sudan, already weakened by the victories of Yohannes, was broken by the Mahdists on 5 November 1882, when an Egyptian army of 10,000 men with thirty-six guns under the command of Hicks Pasha was encircled by a probably smaller Mahdist force near El Obeid, and annihilated. The British at last became aware to some degree of what was happening in the Sudan. Plans were hastily drafted to evacuate the surviving Egyptian garrisons in the south and east. Gordon was sent to Khartoum to arrange withdrawal from the Sudan itself, and negotiatons were opened with Yohannes to cover the retreat of the Egyptians from Kassala and the Red Sea littoral, offering the Emperor, as an inducement, the privilege of occupying the areas being abandoned by the Egyptians, if he could hold them against the Mahdists, and at the same time allowing him free transit through the port of Massawa, on condition of its being placed under British protection.

These would have been attractive offers if Yohannes had been in a position to take advantage of them. However, they implied

the end of Italian ambitions in the Red Sea, and as such they indicated again the embarrassing limitations of Italian power. The fact was that Abyssinia counted for more at the time than Italy. Yohannes ruled over a nation of barely two million, whereas Tewfik had five million subjects, and the Sudan probably many more; but Yohannes could deploy armies of 100,000 or more formidable fighters, which made him the most powerful military factor on the spot in Africa.

Italy had to do something to redress the balance. News of the massacre of the explorer Gustav Bianchi and other members of the Giulietti expedition in the hinterland of Assab provided Mancini with an opportune excuse for military intervention. Paget was asked to define Britain's attitudes to Italian occupation of the whole Red Sea littoral and a punitive expedition was assembled at Naples. The British welcomed this display of white solidarity by agreeing on 22 December, and without informing Yohannes, that they had no objection to Italy's annexing the whole area between Massawa and Beilul; and on 17 January 1885, 840 troops sailed on the *Gottard* for Massawa, under the command of Admiral Caimi. The Italians were on the march again, for the first time in nineteen years. They would need to do better this time.

They particularly needed to do better because they were at last playing a lone hand. Germany and Austria had not been informed of the enterprise; relations with France had been at breaking point ever since 1881; Russia could never be counted on to give encouragement to one of Austria's allies; and the British had shown that they were at least as willing to deal with Abyssinia as with Italy, and to betray both, if need be. But the extent of Italy's isolation itself made the venture all the more significant. It was fifteen inglorious and unruly years since Rome had been seized as a symbol of Italian unification. It was high time that an Italian government did something in the field of foreign affairs to make its people proud of the Kingdom. It was also virtually their last chance. Other colonists were already descending on Africa for the kill – the 'scramble' had begun. Germany had already established protectorates over the Cameroons and the vast expanse of south-west Africa; the Spanish had seized Rio Muni and Ifni, and extended a protectorate over the coastline south of the Canaries; a huge free state had bloomed in the Congo under the enterprise of King Leopold of Belgium; the Portuguese were thrusting inland from the Angolan coast; and the British were beginning to establish themselves on the ruins of Egyptian power in Harrar, on the Gulf of Aden, and in Bechuanaland in the south. Italy was almost too late.

Surprisingly enough, all went well at first. Caimi arrived in Massawa on 5 February 1885, just eleven days after the fall of Khartoum had made the British more ready than ever to welcome any friendly European presence in East Africa, and then came General Gene from Assab with 3,000 more men. Having unceremoniously bundled out the departing Egyptians, they promptly offered to help the British to reconquer the Sudan in return for being allowed to take over Harrar. But London was in no mood for any further military adventures as yet. The Italian offer was declined, which left Gene's troops roosting uncomfortably on their microscopic bridgeheads, while the tide of conquest rolled over the continent. And it was not only the other European Powers which were on the march. African rulers were no more restrained. The rule of the Mahdi swept north towards the Egyptian border, in the wake of Tewfik's fleeing garrisons, and east again towards Yohannes' capital of Gondar; the borders of the Ethiopian Empire extended rapidly as Menelik began to advance his rule from the Shoan highlands south to Lake Rudolf and west towards the Indian Ocean.

At the least it might be presumed that Yohannes now had more than enough to concern him, without bothering about Italian incursions in the north. The Italians accordingly began to probe inland from Assab, to gain control of the caravan routes to the coast. But their temerity showed remarkably the mobility, fighting qualities and sheer mass of the man power available to a ruler of Abyssinia. Yohannes swiftly despatched two armies, one under Ras Adar to repel the Mahdists, and one under the skilled Ras Alula to deal with the European trespassers. He had in fact slightly overreached himself. Ras Adar was forced to withdraw after a furious encounter with the Moslem invaders. But Alula, with 10,000 men, trapped an Italian expedition of 460 at Dogali and massacred nearly all of them. Italy had been beaten again.

But this time it did not matter. There was no disgrace in losing against odds of twenty to one. Indeed, the totality of the disaster served to boost Italian morale and national pride, since it could be shown that Italian soldiers had fought literally to last man against impossible numbers, and had died with their arms in their hands. And there was no question now that Italy could exact vengeance. The stimulus of French enmity, inflamed in November 1886 by the breaking-off of commercial relations between the two countries, had led to one of the periodic renaissances of Italian military power. The Kingdom was once again unquestionably the third naval Power in the world. It was also able to mobilize an army, for home defence at least, almost as large as that of Germany, and far larger than that of any other European Power except Russia. The prestige of such a nation was not to be affected by the loss of 430 heroes in East Africa. An expeditionary force of 20,000 men was assembled in January 1888; Menelik, who had himself mobilized 89,000 fighting men, counted the odds again, and decided to welcome the Italians as allies in a common Christian front against the Mahdists;[17] and on 16 June 1888 Italy formally annexed Massawa by force of arms. The tricolour flew along 250 miles of the African coast, facing the most dangerous native forces in the Continent.

The Italians were once again only just in time. A weird new factor was about to intrude itself into Abyssinian politics. A Russian explorer, Nicolai Ivanovitch Ashinov, had apparently managed to get himself thrown out of Assab, along with the Egyptians, when Admiral Caimi's men arrived there in February 1885. Ashinov had subsequently arranged a visit by Abyssinian clergy to Russia, and had actually gained the approval of the

French and Russian governments for an abortive colonizing venture, which was intended to bring to an end Anglo-German-Italian penetration and exploitation. But the little expedition was tracked through the Red Sea by an Italian gunboat, and refused permission to land at Massawa. The Russians then disembarked on the coast of French Somaliland, only to be driven out by the naval bombardment of a French squadron. The 'first and last Russian settlement in Africa' thus came to an end.[18] But the Russians had been on shore long enough for Menelik of Shoa to pay his respects and to commence a relationship with St Petersburg which complicated East African affairs for the next fifty years.

For Menelik's hour had come at last. In March 1889 Yohannes, the most harassed of Abyssinian rulers until Haile Selassie, once more led his forces against the Mahdists. In a desperate struggle at Gallabat, the Abyssinians determinedly carried the Mahdist positions until Yohannes himself fell fatally wounded. On the news of the defeat and death of the Emperor, Menelik immediately established himself as Yohannes' successor. At forty-five years of age, the Shoan leader was the very model of a high-born adventurer. Burly, genial, softly spoken, watchful, immensely intelligent, wholly untrustworthy, and a consummate artist in the use of both humour and cruelty, Menelik could have won distinction in any age or in any profession. He was to become the most successful of African rulers ever to challenge the might of a foreign invader.

Menelik had already shown his willingness to negotiate with the Italians when he suspended his preparations to challenge their landing at Massawa. Now he even went as far as to sign a treaty with them, which undoubtedly meant that one of the signatories would be subordinated to the other. The strange thing was, however, that it was not made clear which of the parties was to have the upper hand. Under the terms of the Treaty of Uccalli of 2 May 1889, Menelik agreed to abolish slavery in his vastly enlarged dominions in return for a gift of 8,000 modern rifles from the Italians; he also agreed to make use of the good offices of the King of Italy in his dealings with foreign Powers. But the implications of the words used to convey the nature of Menelik's agreement differed significantly in the two authentic texts of the Treaty. The Italian text unquestionably implied Menelik's consent to having Abyssinia's foreign relations conducted by the King of Italy, whereas the Amharic text equally clearly expressed Menelik's condescension, as if he were merely availing himself of services provided by the King of Italy, who was to him a sort of feudal vassal.

The likelihood of disagreement between the two parties was obvious. Italy naturally assumed that it had effectively imposed a protectorate on Abyssinia by assuming control of that state's foreign affairs; Menelik on the other hand could claim with equal justice that he had only agreed to make use of the services of the Italians for as long as it suited the needs of Abyssinia. But linguistic difficulties are always unimportant: there was no mere problem of interpretation at stake. What mattered was that the Italians proposed to absorb Abyssinia into their colonial empire as quickly as they could contrive to do so, and Menelik intended to stop them for as long as he could.

Menelik was not on his own any more: the Italians themselves had been unwise enough to let him have 8,000 new rifles, and other European Powers were prepared to be far more generous. And not only this, but the crackbrained Ashinov expedition was having its reverberations. In October 1889 the Archbishop of Kiev sent Lieutenant Vasili Mashkov to seek an audience with Menelik, with a view to uniting the Russian and Abyssinian Churches, which might have presented serious difficulties, had not an alignment of Russian and Abyssinian interests in foreign policy been easy to contrive.[19] Italy was effectively allied with Britain in Africa against France, and Russia was challenging British imperial interests all the way from the Aegean Sea to the Himalayas.[20] Menelik accordingly cultivated his Russian acquaintance, while 55,759 Italian troops poured through the Suez Canal, to complete the subjugation of Eritrea in the north.[21] He even held his peace when the government in

1a. The war with Turkey, 1911–13: Italian soldiers leaving Rome for Tripoli
Radio Times Hulton Picture Library

1b. The war with Turkey: Italian heavy guns
Radio Times Hulton Picture Library

2a. First World War: anti-aircraft gun above Caporetto

Imperial War Museum

2b. First World War: The Udine-Codrinto road during the Italian retreat after Caporetto, 1917

Radio Times Hulton Picture Library

Rome sent an expedition to occupy the town of Adowa, fifty miles within the borders of Abyssinian territory, to reaffirm their authority over their old conqueror and Viceroy of that region, Ras Alula. Then in April 1891 Tsar Nicholas II sent Menelik 80,000 repeating rifles as a personal gift, and Russia's newly found allies and Italy's long-standing rivals, the French, weighed in with a further 80,000 rifles, some machine-guns, and a million rounds of ammunition. Menelik now had enough modern infantry weapons to equip an army of nearly 200,000, at a time when the Mahdi was still holding out against Britain and Egypt with barely a tenth as many riflemen.

Challenge was immediately followed by response. On 15 April 1892 the British government at last recognized the whole of Abyssinia as a sphere of Italian interest. Menelik at once denounced all foreign claims to his dominions, whereupon the Italians reacted by ordering further incursions into Abyssinian territory, and inducing the Sultan of Zanzibar to hand over control of his Somali ports to Italian administrators. Prime Minister Giolitti affirmed in Rome that Abyssinia would indeed remain within the orbit of Italian influence, and that an external protectorate would be maintained over Menelik. The Abyssinian ruler's next move was to denounce Uccalli. The Italian government made a feeble attempt to stave off a showdown by sending Dr Traversi of the Geographical Society on a goodwill visit to Menelik, to offer him two million rounds of ammunition if he would accept the protectorate. The predictable consequence was that Menelik rejected the protectorate, and kept the ammunition. It was to prove useful two years later.

Menelik had outplayed the Italians at their own speciality of evasive diplomacy. But Giolitti still had grounds for confidence. On 20 December 1893 Italian troops operating from Eritrea boldly drove an army of 10,000 Mahdists from the field at Agordat, thus achieving the first decisive victory yet won by Europeans against the Sudanese revolutionaries, and the first victory of any kind yet won by the army of the Kingdom of Italy against anybody. Italian militarism gained its most characteristic symbol in the image of the Bersagliero on colonial service, his pith helmet adorned with black plumes, facing a savage enemy on an exotic terrain with his battle cry commemorating the name of Italy's first colonial beach-head: 'Eia, eia, eia, Alala!'. The home population was quick to catch the flame. New classes of conscripts responded eagerly to the call to the colours.

No limits were to be placed on the extent and cost of the war to defend the colonies. But the Italians had no conception of what the cost of a successful war against Abyssinia could be; and the cost was mounting all the time. In July 1894 Russia also denounced the Treaty of Uccalli; an Ethiopian mission was received in St Petersburg with honours more lavish than those accorded any previous foreign visitors in Russian history; and Tsar Nicholas approved a further shipment to Menelik through the port of French Somaliland, of 100,000 rifles and twelve million rounds. General Baratieri could command in Italian East Africa perhaps 30,000 Italian troops and 15,000 native Askaris. He would have needed about four times that number to subdue Menelik. No colonial empire had ever raised such an expedition before. The British admittedly were to despatch about a quarter of a million regulars overseas during the three years of the South African war,[22] but the British had the time; they had the resources of an immense empire; and their command of the seas ensured that they had no need to be concerned about leaving the Home Islands exposed to a foreign invasion. Italy had neither time, resources nor security.

And yet it still looked as if the Italian numbers and fighting skills might be sufficient. Baratieri sallied out against the Mahdists again, on 12 July 1894, and drove them from Kassala, killing 2,600 of the enemy for a loss of only twenty-eight Italian dead, in what was by far the most impressively one-sided victory won by Europeans against the Dervishes. He followed this up a year later with another successful offensive action at Debra Aila against an Abyssinian army far larger than his own, commanded by Menelik's vassal, Ras Magascia. But Baratieri did not know what he was up against. He later pleaded in his own defence that as Menelik himself did not know how many warriors followed his banners he could not possibly hope to get such information.[23] But Menelik did not need to know: he had numbers to spare. Baratieri had not. This should have been sufficiently indicated on 17 December 1895, when an Abyssinian army about 30,000 strong trapped 2,450 Italians at Ambu Alagi, and killed or took prisoner 1,320 of them. Baratieri was still prepared to gamble on his chances, however. In a singularly Latin challenge to destiny he divided his forces, leaving 30,000 to contain the revolt now simmering in his rear, and pushed on defiantly to relieve Adowa with only 10,596 men, marching by night, in wholly unsuitable uniforms designed for the European winter, over quite unfamiliar terrain, in a country where he could not even understand the road signs.[24] It was a strategy that might have worked against leaderless savages. But the fact was that Abyssinian rulers had been accustomed for centuries to organize and deploy armies massive even by European standards. This was not the situation anywhere else in Africa, but then the Italians had not been fighting anywhere else in Africa. They should have learned by now.

Their education was completed the following day. Menelik rushed upon them with a gigantic assembly of over 100,000 riflemen. It was the greatest of African battles. Menelik's cohorts sustained 20,000 casualties, and when silence fell over the field of Adowa Baratieri's army had been almost completely destroyed. 6,889 of the Italians and their native Askaris were dead, 1,000 wounded, and 2,000 taken prisoner.

Adowa was not quite the greatest of colonial disasters – the British had suffered worse on occasion in Afghanistan – but it did at least ensure that the conquest of Abyssinia was completely off anybody's schedule for the time being, it being obvious that Menelik now had the power to defy any European imperialist. And it genuinely demoralized the Italian public, who had been rejoicing in the record of easy and brilliant colonial victories, the more gratifying because they were the first their army had ever enjoyed, and who had not been prepared in the least by their political leaders for a setback in Africa, let alone total disaster. In the words of two commentators, 'Adowa aroused all the morbid sentimentality of a people not yet accustomed to national life.'[25] It certainly affected ardent patriots like D'Annunzio as 'a shameful scar', the mark of which was to be healed only forty years later, by Mussolini's legions. It also brought down Crispi, and it halted dead in its tracks any military plans for expanding Italian rule in East Africa by force. And, most important of all, it reduced miserably the area and population over which Italy could claim to exercise direct or indirect rule.

It did not, however, affect in any significant degree Italy's capacity to hold on to other colonial territories. Menelik might be able to ambush and destroy an Italian army in the field, but he could not advance openly against one unless he could count on a numerical advantage of something like ten to one. And as there was no possibility of his rallying half a million warriors around his banners, there was no chance of his over-running Eritrea. The fundamental strength of the Italian position was affirmed almost at once. The British had tentatively advanced towards Dongola, on their way to Khartoum, to relieve pressure on the Italians after Adowa, for fear that Eritrea might be about to fall to the Mahdists. But their help was not needed. Baratieri's successor, General Baldessera, swept the Dervishes away from Mount Mocram barely a month after Adowa, killing 800 of an invading force of 5,000. He then won a brisk series of skirmishes which had the effect of finally convincing Menelik that he should count himself lucky to have preserved the independence of his own empire.

Baldessera was indeed strong and competent enough to have forced Menelik to risk battle in the open field again, and thus to have reversed the decision of Adowa. But the Italian government and people had not yet recovered their taste for large-scale military enterprises. They contented themselves with completing the take-over of the Indian Ocean littoral from the Sultan of Zanzibar, thus cutting Abyssinia finally off the sea,[26] at the same time that they negotiated with Menelik the abrogation of the

Treaty of Uccalli. The Shoan Emperor, for his part, cordially assured the Italians of his future goodwill towards their nation, cut the right hands and left feet off four hundred captured Askaris to serve as mementoes of his victory at Adowa, and began assiduously entertaining new Russian military and medical expeditions. Meanwhile, the Mahdist challenge dissolved at Omdurman, when an Anglo-Egyptian army of 23,000 encountered a half-armed Dervish rally of barely twice their own strength, and massacred them in country supremely suitable for the use of machine-guns. There was no comparison between this kind of fighting and the campaigns of Agordat and Kassala, Debra Aila and Ambu Alagi. But the Union Jack had been carried triumphantly back into East Africa. There was silence in the Shoan Highlands.

2 : Challenge from the Mediterranean

RUSSIAN and French guns, Italian misjudgment and the talents of Menelik imposed peace at Adowa for forty years. They could not, however, affect Italy's capacity to influence decisively the balance of forces in Europe. The young kingdom was still admittedly the weakest of the Great Powers: Italian military expenditure was barely a third that of Germany, Russia or France; and only marginally greater than that of Austria-Hungary; its military man power had fallen below the Austrian level; and the former proud boasts of maritime glory had been abandoned as the volume of Italian merchant and naval shipping fell to sixth place in the world's lists.[1] But there was still an immense gulf between the defence capacity of Italy and that of any European state other than the five Great Powers. And there was no doubt that Italian power aligned to either of the developing alliance groups would make the strength of that group overwhelming. What was still uncertain was where Italy's natural inclination as an ally would be directed.

For Italy remained the joker in the European pack. Its colonial interests involved it in difficulties with France; its strategic interests clashed directly with those of Austria; and its relations with France's ally Russia or with Austria's ally Germany were naturally imperilled in consequence. Only with England had there been a cordial working relationship, based on mutual support in East Africa, and even this now seemed to have outlived its usefulness. But it had left a legacy. Back in July 1890, as the Italians established themselves in Eritrea in a position which would cover the flank of a British advance against the Mahdists, Crispi had become concerned over the prospect that the French protectorate over Tunis might be extended into outright annexation on the death of the present Bey. He accordingly proposed to Lord Salisbury that such an extension of French imperial control along the Mediterranean littoral might require Italy to annex Tripoli to safeguard its own position in the area.[2] Salisbury was disposed to conciliate the Italians and he assured Crispi that an Italian occupation of Tripoli would indeed become 'absolutely necessary' when any such alteration took place in the Mediterranean, for Britain was not going to accept that the Mediterranean should become a French lake. But he also indicated to Crispi that an attack on Tripoli would be the signal for the dismemberment of Turkey, so that Italy should not anticipate matters, but should wait until the French had effected the alteration that Crispi was concerned about.[3]

Salisbury's predictions were quite correct. Another military defeat would be certain to bring an end to the Turkish Empire in Europe, and take the lid off the cauldron of the Balkans, where all the countries were seething with rapacious nationalism. And this would mean that the Austrian and Russian Empires would virtually be compelled to intervene to safeguard their own irreconcileable economic and strategic interests in the region. But they would not be allowed to do so on their own. Britain had shown already in 1877 that it would fight to keep the Russians away from the Straits, which were a vital part of the imperial lifeline to India. And military talks were already projected between Russia and France, as a result of the economic strife between Russia and Germany in 1888, so that it was not likely that the French would allow their only prospective European ally to be defeated, any more than it was likely that the Germans would allow Russia to roll over Austria and leave them also without a reliable continental ally. The partnerships might change, but the result would be the same. An Italian victory in Tripoli was likely to mean the dissolution of Turkish authority in Europe; this would necessarily involve intervention by Austria and Russia; and intervention by Austria and Russia could hardly fail to involve every other major power in a European and possibly a global war. It was a high price to pay for the restoration of Italy's national prestige.

For this was all that there was at stake in Tripoli itself. There was no booming Italian community there, as there had been in Tunis: there were barely 4,000 Christians living in all of Turkish North Africa, and only about 850 of these were Italians.[4] Italy had an important trading interest, but even then the total value of Italian commerce with Tripoli was lower than that of either Britain or Turkey. But the strategic implication was obvious. French extension into Tripoli, coupled with Austrian control of the eastern seaboard of the Adriatic, would make Italy just about the most thoroughly encircled nation on earth. No Great Power could ever allow itself to lose strategic defensibility in this way – still less could a Power wishing to establish itself as one of the Great. The only question seemed to be whether it was reasonable for Europe to allow Italy to confirm its Great Power status at such a price.

The real question, however, was whether Europe could stop the Italians from doing anything they wanted to. The quest for Security among the Great Powers was reaching a point of urgency unknown since the defeat of Napoleon. France and Russia had concluded an alliance against Germany in 1894; serious tension had developed between Germany and Britain because of the decision of Kaiser Wilhelm II to build a High Seas fleet, designed to make Germany the second naval power in the world; and British anxieties had been increased by the discovery that their fleet in the Pacific was outgunned by the French and Russian squadrons there, at a time when the prestige of the British army was being shattered by the Boers in South Africa. Everybody had suddenly become vulnerable, and in this situation, everyone needed an ally. Italy could now bargain for a free hand in Africa, even if the consequence of its action was likely to be a conflict which would spread from the Balkans to all the Great Powers of Europe.

There were at last men in Rome who were prepared to play to win with the cards available to them. After Adowa, Emilio Visconti Venosta had been called to the Foreign Ministry. He was aged sixty-seven, and had served three previous terms of office at the Consulta (the Italian Foreign Office). Over the next four years, he negotiated an agreement with the French, conceding French rights in Morocco, but reserving the corresponding right of Italy to extend its own influence in Tripoli and Cyrenaica, should France alter the actual political and territorial status of Morocco. He also managed to reach an understanding with the Austrians on the establishment of a neutral and independent Albania, should Turkish rule collapse in the Balkans. This was a wise move, which served to redeem the folly of Admiral Felice Canevaro, who, on replacing Venosta as Foreign Minister in 1899, had used his position to send three Italian ships to demand a naval base and extra-territorial concessions from the government of China. Canevaro's bold venture of sending the tricolour into the Pacific might well have succeeded had he not been compelled by the British to abandon the idea of using force on the Chinese, whom Salisbury was seeking to conciliate at the time. The result was the familiar Italian fiasco. But it was the last one. A year later it was the turn of the British to be humiliated, when British diplomats were besieged in Peking by the Boxers, and the British government was compelled to appeal to the other Powers to rescue them, being itself helpless because of its involvements in South Africa. Venosta triumphantly responded by sending an expedition of 2,000 men and six ships, allegedly 'to defend the sacred rights of oppressed humanity'.[5] This description might have been more fittingly applied to the Boxers than to the diplomats. But then, neither was the Italian intervention a very notable military exercise. Only about fifty of Venosta's legionnaires actually participated in the relief of Peking, compared with 10,000 Japanese, 4,000 Russians, 3,000 Englishmen, 2,000 Americans, 800 French and 200 Germans.[6] No Italian blood was shed. Nevertheless, the enterprise reaffirmed Italy's position in the company of the

Imperial Powers; it enhanced Venosta's prestige; and it gained for his Kingdom the concession port of Tien-Tsin, in place of San Mun, which Canevaro had tried to commandeer in 1899. The tricolour now flew in three continents.

Visconti Venosta left the Consulta in 1901. Nobody had ever served the Kingdom better. He was succeeded by a man strikingly dissimilar in temperament, but admirably equipped to build on the foundations that he had left. Giulio Prinetti possessed all of Crispi's imperial vision and Visconti Venosta's dedication, amplified by the vehement emotionalism and wheeler-dealing zeal of a strident Lombard businessman. His readiness to explore all avenues of protifiable negotiation was made the stronger by his personal aversion for the Triple Alliance, now due for renewal. Prinetti demanded forthrightly from German Foreign Minister Bernhard von Bulow that Germany and Austria should undertake to give Italy a free hand in Tripoli, on payment for continued Italian allegiance to the Alliance. Bulow, ever a man to meet bluster with more bluster, unconditionally rejected Prinetti's demands, just as he also torpedoed the talks then in train between Britain and Germany, by insisting that any arrangements between the two countries should be extended to include Austria as well. The results were wholly unsatisfactory for Germany in both cases. Britain turned to Japan, and thence to France and even to Russia. Italy also turned to France and Russia, but not until after Prinetti had managed to extract a sufficiently satisfactory concession from his uncongenial allies. The Triple Alliance was renewed in Berlin on 28 June 1902, without any formal alteration in its terms; the idea of the free hand in all circumstances was refused by the Germans and Austrians; but Italy's partners did agree not to interfere if Italy found it necessary to effect a change in the political situation in North Africa, in order to protect its own interests. Prinetti had now got all that he really wanted out of Berlin and Vienna. And two days later he extended Visconti Venosta's accord with Paris, reaching agreement on a definition of French interests in Morocco and Italian interests in Tripoli, in return for a promise that Italy would observe neutrality if France were compelled to go to war in defence of its honour and security, or as a consequence of its having been the victim of direct or indirect aggression.

Nations do not usually go to war unless it is in defence of their own honour and security, and as Italy was no longer threatened it could not now be counted on by its Triple Alliance partners to stand by them in the event of a war with France, just as it had already made clear that it would not stand by them in a war against Britain. The precise nature of the services which Italy could be counted on to provide in defence of the Alliance was becoming a little hard to define. The most that could really be hoped was that Italy would at least never become an active ally of France; but the only way that the Germans and Austrians could assure themselves of even this much comfort was by giving the Italians no reason to doubt that they could rely on the support of their allies if they were to get themselves involved in war with France. Italy had won all round. The country which had been accustomed to bring back from the arena of international diplomacy nothing but demoralizing set-backs had emerged as the one Great Power in Europe with practically unfettered freedom of action. Italy could send the world to war with impunity.

It was soon clear that this was exactly what would happen. Austria had been able to contemplate the disintegration of the Turkish Empire in Europe with a reasonable degree of calm at the turn of the century when its own position in the Balkans seemed absolutely secure. Italy was committed to neutrality by the terms of the Triple Alliance; Serbia was a docile economic satellite of Vienna; and the link with the Black Sea was completed by the adherence of Romania to the Austro-German compact. But all this had dissolved by 1903. Italy was riding free between Paris and Berlin; the co-operative Obrenovich dynasty in Belgrade had been replaced by the chauvinistic and Russophile Karageorgeviches in a palace revolution involving atrocities impressive even by Balkan standards; and the prospect of gradual and peaceful Austrian progress to Salonika, across the lines of any Russian advance, was gone forever. The Austro-German dilemma was complete. It was now even more likely that Italian action against Tripoli would precipitate international war in the Balkans; and it was even more important for the Central Powers not to alienate the Italians completely, in case they found themselves faced with war against France and Russia at the same time.

The fact was that the indiscretion of Bulow and a palace revolution in Belgrade had cost the Central Powers the diplomatic initiative in Europe. It was not only in Rome that politicians felt free to manoeuvre. Italy had secured international recognition of its freedom to move against Tripoli if the French altered the political *status quo* in North Africa; and the French could feel free to make what alterations they chose since the Italians and the British could both be counted on not to oppose them. London and Paris reached agreement on colonial spheres of interest in 1904, just as Paris and Rome had done in 1900 and 1902. As a result of this agreement, the French imposed a programme of reforms on the Sultan of Morocco. By March, however, Kaiser Wilhelm had landed in Tangier, thus provoking an international crisis. His declared purpose was to affirm the principle of a free and independent Morocco, open to the peaceful competition of all nations; to insist on his resolve to defend German interests in the territory; and to caution the Sultan about the need to proceed carefully with the required reforms[7]. Germany's real intention was of course to force upon France a series of humiliations which would have the effect of breaking the Anglo-French accord, since they would present the French with the prospect of having to fight in situations in which they could not count on British support.[8] It was the kind of tortuously ingenious policy that could have recommended itself to no one but the frivolous Bulow, or the perverse Friedrich von Holstein, the official head of the German Foreign Office. There was no way in which it could be made to work in practice. Even the Austrians recognized the folly of trying to insist on international rights in Morocco. It was quite plain that the only people with genuine interests there were the French, who wanted to annex the place, and the Italians, who wanted the French to extend their power in north-west Africa, so that they would have an excuse to move against Tripoli. The Italians admirably tried to avoid embarrassment by opposing the whole idea of a conference, and were to some extent let off the hook by the almost equally embarrassed Austrians, who tried to merge the reality of a Franco-German confrontation in an amorphous international discussion.

Vienna's fears proved to be completely justified. Germany was the isolated nation in the conference held in Algeciras between January and April 1906. Nobody was prepared to believe that Kaiser Wilhelm had any altruistic motive in seeking to preserve the integrity of Morocco, and mutual suspicion of Berlin's intentions actually drove the British and French closer together. At the same time, the weakness of the Triple Alliance was manifested by the unwillingness of both Austria and Italy to support the German position. All that Bulow really succeeded in doing was to get his proposal accepted that the police in Morocco should be subject to the supervision of the Diplomatic Corps in Tangier. This admittedly would make it more difficult for the French to establish a full protectorate over the country, as they had done in the case of Tunis; but against this it was agreed that the police should be subject solely to French inspectors in four ports, to French and Spanish jointly in Tangier and Casablanca, and to Spanish alone in only two other places. There was thus little doubt that the apparatus of law enforcement in Morocco would be applied generally in a manner consonant with French wishes. But these matters were now really of little interest in Berlin. What was important for Germany's leaders was to recover from the state of virtual diplomatic isolation into which they had managed to engineer themselves at Algeciras, where virtually nobody had been prepared unreservedly to support the German position. And Vienna had shown little more faith than Rome. But the Germans recognized a basic difference between the posture of their two Treaty partners. Italy would not oppose France in North Africa, because it had already recognized French interest in Morocco for its own ends; and it would never risk a war with Britain because this would expose Italy to blockade and assault by overwhelming sea power. Austria, on the other hand, had no such reason to placate the French or fear the British. Kaiser Wilhelm accordingly congratulated the Austrians on the brilliant support which they had in fact failed to give him at Algeciras, and contrasted their alleged loyalty with the unreliable policy of Italy, even offering to assist Austria in administering a salutary lesson to Italy, 'perhaps even with sword in hand'.[9]

This was presumably intended only to reassure the Austrians. The last thing in the world that Germany needed in 1906 was more enemies. It was one thing to recognize the serious limitations of Italy's uses as an ally, and quite another deliberately to drive Italy into the enemy camp. But as it happened Conrad von Hotzendorf, the new Chief of the Austrian General Staff, was already considering war with Italy as a prerequisite for the achievement of Austria's goals of foreign policy. This indeed may well have been true, in so far as these goals involved complete Austrian domination of the Adriatic littoral and its hinterland. And in the meantime the Italians were closing ranks ever more impressively with the French and British. The three countries reached an agreement in December 1906 on their respective spheres of interest in Abyssinia, in anticipation of the time when that state would revert to anarchy on the death of the ailing Menelik. Unilateral intervention was ruled out, but it was recognized that the preservation of Eritrea and Italian Somaliland required that the north, south and east of Abyssinia should be regarded as a potential sphere of Italian influence, and that Italy was to be allotted the right to a territorial connection between its existing colonies, cutting across Abyssinia west of Addis Ababa.

Menelik of course was not dead yet, and the Italians accordingly sought to improve their existing relations with the still viable African state by concluding a commercial treaty with him. Meanwhile, Italian capital poured into Albania and Dalmatia, moving Conrad to insist ever more vehemently upon the necessity to remove by force the threat of Italian rivalry in the Balkans. Such a decisive action was scarcely practicable for the divided and ponderous administration of the Habsburg Empire, but there did seem to be more pacific and unobstrusive ways of securing the Balkan domination conducive to both the prestige and the economic development of Austria. On 1 December 1907, the Austrians announced their intention of annexing the provinces of Bosnia and Hercegovina, which they had been administering ever since 1878. It was hard to see how such a move, which was purely legalistic, could alter the real position in the Balkans, but it could be regarded as a preparatory step towards effective action by the Empire against Serbia. And there was no doubt that it altered the *status quo* established by the Congress of Berlin, and thereby opened the possibility of new negotiations on the frontiers of south-eastern Europe.

The Russians were naturally the first to raise the issue of a renegotiation. On 2 July 1908 they indiscreetly offered to recognize Austria's annexation on the provinces, in return for Austrian recognition of Russia's interests in the Dardanelles. The Austrians were not responsive to this, but the Italians were prompt to discern an advantage for themselves in Russian concern with the fate of the Balkans. Negotiations between Rome and St Petersburg began secretly in December, on the preliminary basis of a mutual agreement to preserve the integrity of Turkey, to apply the principle of nationality to any future solution of the Balkan problem, and to reach mutual consent before either party recognized further Austrian incursions in the area.

One such incursion was very clearly in the minds of Austria's military leaders. Austrian officers called emotionally for the Emperor to lead them to war against Serbia, to salvage the honour of the Empire.[10] Not only did the proposal have many practical considerations to recommend it, it was made more reasonable still by an assurance given to Conrad on 21 January 1909 by his opposite number in Berlin, Helmuth von Moltke, that Germany would stand beside Austria, sword in hand, if the other were to find itself at war with Russia as a result of a punitive assault on Serbia. This undertaking went immeasurably far beyond the purely defensive provisions of the Dual Alliance. Germany's army, if not its government, was giving Austria a green light for aggression in the Balkans. It was easy to see why, when one considered that German investments in Austria-Hungary amounted to something like three billion marks,[11] returns for which could be guaranteed only if the expansion of the Austrian economy continued. And Austria's expansion was dependent upon the unimpeded exploitation of the resources of the Danubian basin, as well as free access to the world outside for the products of this exploitation. The way ahead for Austria was through Salonika, and the road to Salonika passed through Serbia.[12] There was also no doubt that Germany's diplomatic position would be enhanced if its ally proved capable of carrying out a successful campaign of aggression. A Power apparently incapable of giving offence is a Power that positively invites humiliation and even attack.

But the Austrians continued to pursue a positively conciliatory line. Having annexed the two provinces, they then unilaterally withdrew their garrisons from the narrow Sanjak of Novi-Bazar, lying between Serbia and Montenegro, and apparently serving as a sally port for a Habsburg raid on Salonika. It was a concession which enabled the Russians to withdraw from the affair without total loss of face; but it did not, however, prevent the Russians and Italians from ratifying the Racconigi Agreement of 24 October 1909. This treaty not only cemented their agreement on the original proposals regarding the integrity of Turkey, the application of the principle of nationality and mutual consent in respect to Austrian disturbances of the *status quo,* it also joined them in an attitude of goodwill towards both Russian activities in the Dardanelles, and Italian activities in Tripoli. Italy had completed its preparations. London, Paris, Berlin,

Vienna and now St Petersburg had all been persuaded to agree over the past nineteen years to condone Italian expansion in Tripoli, as a response to French expansion elsewhere in North Africa. The diplomatic prelude was over. The next step would be up to the army, who had Adowa to avenge, and the navy, whose traditions began with Lissa.

The abandonment of the Sanjak did not exhaust Austria's readiness to conciliate. Negotiations had begun between Rome and Vienna even while the Racconigi Agreement was being finalized, culminating on 19 December, when the two partners of the Triple Alliance agreed to adopt the principle of mutual agreement on any moves to change the *status quo* in the Balkans. The Austrians also undertook not to reoccupy the Sanjak until they had reached an accord with Italy.

They could indeed hardly have done less if they wished to remain consistent with the preservation of the Triple Alliance. Italian interests in the Balkans were obviously even more urgent than Russian ones. Russia was after all separated from the Aegean by the fourfold barrier of Romania, Bulgaria, Turkey-in-Europe, and Greece. But the Adriatic littoral was vital to the strategic security of the Kingdom of Italy; Victor Emmanuel was married to a Montenegrin princess, Elena; and the Balkans had become Italy's major area of foreign investment. On all indications, Austria's interests in south-eastern Europe would collide with those of Italy even before they encountered Russia's.

They could not collide too soon for Conrad von Hotzendorf. The submissive accords of December moved him yet again to urge war against Austria's ally, and an earthquake at Messina seemed to him to provide a highly suitable opportunity to attack. His enthusiasm was made the keener by the fact that Italy was the one country against which the multiracial Austrian army could be deployed with confidence. In the first place, the Italians were the only people against whom Austrian armies had fought successfully for over a hundred years. But more important was the racial factor. The Slav troops of the Empire could not be counted upon to show much enthusiasm for combat with their brother Slavs in Serbia, Montenegro and Russia. And even the Hungarians could hardly be expected to be at their brilliant best in a war which was virtually certain to lead to the incorporation of still more Slavs into the Empire, thus increasing the odds against Magyar domination. It was perhaps hardly a sufficient reason for Austria to go to war with Italy, simply because it was less difficult than going to war with anybody else. But there was no doubt that the prestige of the Habsburg Empire would be strengthened by a successful war against the one country whom almost all its peoples were willing to fight and believed they could defeat. Nor was there any doubt that the Italians presented an ever-increasing challenge to Austrian advances in the Balkans.[13] While all this was being considered, family ties between Italy and Montenegro were reaffirmed by a visit of Victor Emmanuel and Elena to Skopje in August 1910. But Vienna remained virtually incapable of effective action in any direction. There were arguments in any case against splitting the Triple Alliance at just that moment. Spain was reputed to be veering towards an *entente* relationship with Britain, France and Russia. Germany at least had no wish to drive even as unsatisfactory an ally as Italy into the French camp. Then time ran out for Europe.

On 23 September 1911 French forces were moved into Fez, the capital of Morocco. They came at the request of the Sultan, who had found his throne becoming ever more shaky as he attempted to impose the programme of reforms dictated by the French in 1905. The occasion had thus been provided for the Italian assault against Turkey-in-Africa, meditated for the past twenty-one years. For a few months action was delayed by the Germans, appearing once again in their role of defenders of international rights in Africa – they sent a gunboat, *Panther,* sailing dramatically into the port of Agadir. But this second bid to contrive the isolation of France was no more successful than the first, for the Italians openly affirmed that they had no objection to France's annexing Morocco. The Germans had once again achieved their own isolation. Negotiations were entered into, to salvage some profit and prestige from the fiasco, during which it was agreed on 4 September that Germany would recognize a French protectorate over Morocco in return for territorial compensation in the Congo. Twenty-four hours later, the Italian armed forces began autumn manoeuvres.

Albertini remarkably argues that the fact that Italy's army and navy were deployed on field exercises at this time indicates that the Italian government had no preconceived intention of going to war.[14] But this was to be above all else a naval war; and it takes only a radio message to divert ships from their peaceful occasions to an assault on an enemy's shores. The timetable proceeded relentlessly, in any case. A formal protest was sent to Constantinople on 23 September, about the failure of Turkish authorities to protect Italian interests in Tripoli. On 25 September, Ambassador de Martino claimed that the tiny Italian community in Tripoli was being positively threatened by their Turkish neighbours. The only Turkish response was to rush reinforcements to the North African colonies. But the Italians were not to be deterred; they sent an incredibly brutal ultimatum to Constantinople, demanding that Tripoli and Cyrenaica should be abandoned to Italian military occupation within twenty-four hours, and then, on 29 September, the Italian avalanche descended.

Few wars can ever have been fought at such a pace. The Italians displayed as nobody could ever have done before the terrifying mobility of superior sea power, deployed against an enemy deficient in warships, in the days before radar and aircraft could alert shore defences of the approach of a hostile fleet. On the day that war was declared the Italians threw a blockade around Tripoli and Cyrenaica, at the same time sinking a Turkish destroyer and a torpedo-boat, driving the Turkish navy from the Adriatic, and bombarding the Ionian port of Prevesa, into which the Turks had attempted to flee. Five days later Vice-Admiral Faravelli's battleships bombarded the port of Tripoli, while Admiral Cagni landed 1,700 marines, who stormed the defences and held the town until a further 34,000 reinforcements arrived on 8 October. It had taken the Italians barely ten days to gain complete command of the eastern Mediterranean, and to render the conquest of Tripoli inevitable.

This was not the war that Europe had expected. The attack on Prevesa in particular seemed to confirm all the worst apprehensions of Italian plans for conquest in the Balkans. The Germans, indefatigably playing their part as guardians of international order, despatched a cruiser squadron to the Mediterranean, presumably in the hope of deterring their ebullient allies from embarking on too ambitious a war. But the Italians were not to be constrained so easily. While reinforcements poured ashore at Tripoli, Admiral Millo led his ships in a series of lightning raids against three towns whose names were to figure again in the records of Italian military experience, twenty-nine years later. Tobruk was bombarded on 5 October; Derna received the same treatment on the 16th, and was occupied by landing parties on the 18th; and Benghazi fell on 22 October, after a brisk engagement, in which the Italians lost seventy dead, and the defenders over 500.

It was not only on land and sea that the Italians were tasting the unfamiliar joys of triumph in battle. Already in 1909 Giulio Douhet had written advising the army and the navy not to see air power as useful merely in an auxiliary capacity: the air was 'a third brother, younger but not the least important, in the great family of war'.[15] The younger brother's début in North Africa was most impressive. The Italians deployed in all nine aircraft, three dirigibles and thirty-nine airmen in the skies over Libya, which witnessed, in short order, the first aerial reconnaissance over enemy lines, the first experiment in aerial photography, the first bombing raid, the first protest against a bombing raid on the grounds that it violated the rules of civilized war, the first military flight by night, the first leaflet raid, the first bombing attack by dirigibles, the first air transport flight, the first bombing raid by night, and the first casualty of the air war.[16] In Italy, Douhet triumphantly hailed, 'the new Army – of the air;

the new field of battle – of the sky; the new principles of conflict – of air war'.[17] But the struggle for the Mediterranean was not going to be decided this time even by Captain Carlo Piazza, bravely piloting his vintage Bleriot over a concentration of Arab horsemen, or by Lieutenant Gavotti, who dropped four 5-pound hand grenades on the Turkish defences.

It was not easy to see exactly how or where it was going to be decided, and on 27 October European anxieties reached a new pitch when Millo's squadrons demonstrated at the mouth of the Dardanelles, defying the Turks to come and accept battle. The enterprise against Turkey had now developed into a world crisis, which of course was only to have been expected, but European governments during the preceding twenty years had not been remarkable for their perception. Conrad von Hotzendorf at least had an answer. On 4 November he yet again urged that Austria should take advantage of this new Italian preoccupation to settle Latin pretensions in the Balkans permanently. He was not the only person concerned at the implications of Italy's naval war. On 24 November the Italians formally blockaded the Dardanelles, an action which led to strong protests on 30 November from the French and Russians, who had about 150,000 tons of shipping trapped in the Black Sea. Paris and St Petersburg, like Vienna, Berlin and London, had been prepared to condone Italian aggression against Turkey if it was limited to North Africa – they had not imagined that the Italians would dare to bombard Greek ports and close the Dardanelles. The mood of Europe was as conducive as it ever could be to drastic action by Austria; but drastic action was simply out of the question in either Vienna or Budapest. The leaders of the Habsburg Empire had long since grown accustomed to the political and administrative impediments to all vigorous forward policy, to the extent that it was far easier to renounce such policy than to remove the impediments. Conrad was transferred to the post of Inspector-General, which was calculated to keep him away from Vienna and in motion around the periphery of the Empire, until the present disturbances had been settled. The laughing diplomats of Vienna had let another opportunity for a comparatively easy war pass by.

Meanwhile the wild hunt of the Italian navy through the Mediterranean went on. Two motives impelled them to continue. One was the simple gratification of defiant successes, which could wipe away the disgrace of Lissa – the tricolour roamed the seas unchecked, in defiance of the wishes of all the Great Powers of Europe. The other was the fact that the Italians really had no other strategy. Although the North African campaign had begun brilliantly with a series of triumphant strikes from the sea, the occupation of the Libyan hinterland was clearly going to be a different matter. An Arab rising in Tripolitania on 29 October had startled the Italians into ferocious reprisals, reminiscent of the uninhibited slaughter of the Abyssinian campaigns. But guerilla strife continued, and was obviously going to continue, no matter what was done to Turkey. Nor was it easy to see how Turkey could reasonably be dealt with. The European Powers would not have tolerated an invasion of the Balkans or Anatolia, so no decision could be sought by land. And as the Turkish navy was unwilling to come out of port and be destroyed, matters could hardly be brought to a conclusion by sea either. A wild hunt for glory seemed to be the most agreeable way of passing the time, until some other means could be found of bringing the war to an end.

This situation did not by any means demonstrate the incompetence of Italian arms, as has surprisingly been asserted.[18] It merely reflected the difficulty of imposing terms on an enemy who refused all invitations to combat, and whose homeland world opinion would not allow the Italians to attack. But unfortunately world opinion could not stop them doing other things. On Christmas Eve 1911 Italian ships swept through the Suez Canal to the mouth of the Red Sea, bombarded the Yemeni ports of Hodeidah and Sheik-Said, and seized the British ship *Puglia*. They then arrested the French ships *Carthage, Manoula,* and *Tavignano* in the Mediterranean, between 16 and 27 January, claiming the right to confiscate alleged contraband of war. This contraband included a Bleriot aeroplane which an enterprising French aviator proposed to sell to the Turks to restore the balance in the air over Libya. Beirut was bombarded on 25 February, and a Turkish gun-boat sunk in harbour. Then in the boldest strike yet, a great Italian fleet of four battleships and twenty escorting torpedo-boats loomed out of the darkness on 19 April, and began to shell the defences of the Dardanelles.

It is probable that even the huge 17.7-inch guns of the old *Giulio Cesare,* the biggest in the world, did as little damage to the forts as the Turks claimed[19] – the forts certainly did no damage to the Italians. Constantinople's only means of retaliation was to protest to the Powers that the sea route through the Straits would have to remain closed for as long as Italian incursions of this kind made it impossible to guarantee the safety of maritime traffic. The Powers in turn reiterated their demands that the Italians lift the blockade. But the Italians had other plans in mind: Millo's battle squadron headed south, to reappear on 6 May off the islands of Rhodes and Lebda, in the southern Dodecanese. There was a brief struggle for Rhodes, in which the Turks were quickly defeated; by 17 May the Italians had occupied eleven of the twelve islands in the group, leaving only the eastern islet of Castelrosso;[20] and on 19 May the Italian fleet gave in to the protests of Europe and lifted the blockade of the Dardanelles, almost six months after it had first been imposed.

This gesture was well timed. Negotiations were already in train between Rome and London on the definition of spheres of interest in Abyssinia, after the Italians had tried unsuccessfully to reach agreement with the dying Menelik on the demarcation of the Somali border.[21]

The interlude was abruptly terminated on 19 July 1912 when Admiral Millo daringly led a flotilla of eight destroyers into the Dardanelles again, penetrating as far as Chanak, in a gratuitous display of contempt for the Turks, defiance of European opinion, and disregard for the orders of his own government.[22] It was indeed a profitless military exercise, as the

Italians withdrew without even firing shots when the shore defences became aware of their presence. Millo was, none the less, hailed by the Italian Press as the hero who forced the Dardanelles, which he had manifestly not done.[23] What he did contrive to do was raise European irritation with Italy to its highest peak. The Russians, who had hitherto been observing the practice of goodwill required by the Racconigi Agreement, were finding the raids on the Dardanelles intolerable; the French, infuriated at having their ships stopped by the Italian blockade, were preparing actively to challenge their new rival in the Mediterranean; and the mood of the Austrians was being held short of active belligerency mainly by the efforts of their German partners, who hoped that the clash with Franch over the blockade issue might force Italy into a greater dependence on the Triple Alliance – this at least was the possibility which Victor Emmanuel cleverly dangled before Kaiser Wilhelm II. In any case, it was clearly time for Italy to disengage itself from the Turkish war. Negotiations were already under way between the British and French, to arrange for the Royal Navy to close the Channel to belligerent ships, thus allowing the French to mass their own naval strength in the Mediterranean, against the fleets of the Triple Alliance, or perhaps against Italy alone. But the Italians were far from being at the end of their resources. The total military humiliation of Turkey was having the anticipated effect: the Balkans were about to boil over, and all the Italians had to do was to foster the process. Italian arms and finance crossed the Adriatic to Montenegro, where preparations for war were being secretly completed in Cetinje. Austrian Foreign Minister Leopold von Berchtold, mild and conciliatory even by the standards of the Ballplatz (the Austrian Foreign Office), attempted to stave off the impending explosion by urging the Powers to persuade Constantinople not to do anything that might endanger peace in the Balkans.[24] But the Balkans were ready to move, no matter what the Turks might do. On 8 October Montenegro declared war, whereupon the Turks hastened to conclude terms with Italy. The Treaty of Ouchy, signed on 15 October, acknowledging Italian sovereignty over Tripolitania and Cyrenaica and Italian occupation of the Dodecanese as a guarantee of Turkish good behaviour in North Africa, was one of the most swiftly composed treaties on record. Preliminary talks began in the morning, and the cease-fire was agreed upon in the afternoon. But nothing could save the Turkish Empire in Europe.

The problem was to check the tide of Balkan success. Italian Foreign Minister Antonino di San Giuliano, accomplished, courtly and utterly cynical, had assured the French on 9 October that Italy would protect the territorial integrity of Turkey,[25] but this was manifestly impossible. All that San Giuliano really intended to protect was the territorial integrity of Albania, now engulfed by Montenegro and Serbia, and eyed covetously by Greece. On 7 November he warned that Serbia would have to withdraw from Albanian territory, something on which Italy and the Austrian Empire could at last co-operate. Each was utterly opposed to letting Montenegro or Albania fall under the control of the other, but they were both equally opposed to letting them fall under the control of an independent Balkan nation. And so on 26 November Berchtold joined with San Giuliano in expressing support for the idea of an autonomous and independent Albania – a gesture which was of unprecedented cordiality. It was made possible by San Giuliano's intense distrust of the French, now massing their fleet in the Mediterranean, and his consequent readiness to embrace the Triple Alliance as the cornerstone of Italy's security even if adherence to the Alliance meant abandoning all traditional ideas of Italy's national destiny. The Alliance was indeed renewed on 5 December, with extra provisions recognizing Italian sovereignty in Tripolitania and Cyrenaica, and stipulating that this recognition was not to affect any agreement reached among the Alliance partners on the situation in Albania, where at that moment the Serbs were bombarding Valona, still obstinately defended by the Turks.

San Giuliano even attempted to give a military reality to the

Alliance, by proposing that combined naval exercises should be carried out in the Mediterranean, as a warning to the French. He also recommended joint Italian-Austrian action in the Balkans to ensure that Albania should receive the town of Scutari, where another Turkish garrison was still holding out. But the honeymoon was almost over. The Austrians now demanded that Montenegro should hand over to Albania its narrow holding on the Adriatic littoral, which would have had the dual effect of cutting Serbia off from the sea, in case that state were to complete its plans for union with Montenegro, and of bringing the Austrian Empire up to the frontier of Albania, where it would be in a position to challenge Italian influence in Tirana. Even San Giuliano was not prepared to abandon Italian ambitions in the Balkans to such a degree. The Italians expressed themselves opposed both to independent coercive action by Austria, and to parallel action against Montenegro and Albania by the Austrians and themselves. This would have meant a confrontation, but it was again briefly averted by a new manifestation of the Balkan crisis. In June 1913 the Bulgarian Army, without the authority of its king, attacked its former allies in an attempt to seize virtually the whole of Macedonia, thereby interposing a strip of Bulgarian-dominated territory between Serbia and the Aegean Sea.

Luck was not with the Bulgarians. By August they had been beaten back into Thrace, while Macedonia and the Sanjak of Novibazer were partitioned among the victorious Greeks, Serbs and Montenagrins. There had indeed been nothing noteworthy about Bulgarian rapacity, by Balkan standards. They had sought to expand their territory only by about 20 per cent, at most, whereas their conquerors had all doubled their area and numbers in the division of the spoils under the terms of the Treaty of Bucharest in August 1913.[26] But the Balkans had been transformed from essentially unimportant factors in any reckoning of power, to vigorous and aggressive states of the second rank. The Greeks in particular were developing positively imperial characteristics. They had already seized the islands of the northern Sporades, and were agitating for possession of the Dodecanese as well, although these were still being occupied by the Italians.[27] They had also seized the district of Ciamuria in southern Albania, despite the fact that only 9,000 of the 63,000 inhabitants were linguistically Greek, and were being kept out of Valona only by Italian threats.[28]

Something would obviously have to be done about Albania. San Giuliano and Berchtold agreed to establish the strategic little state as an independent principality, having as its sovereign the moderately innocuous and tolerably incompetent young Habsburg, Prince William of Wied.[29] Austria and Italy provided the new sovereign with a loan of £500,000 for initial expenses, and on 17 March he was brought to Durazzo by an Austrian warship. But this was the last move upon which the two Powers were ever to agree. Three weeks later San Giuliano warned Berchtold that Italy would never let the Habsburg Empire reach the Albanian border. And on 18 April Austrian indignation exploded over the discovery that the Italians had been assiduously selling arms to Albania, to help the new principality to defend itself against Habsburg encroachments, and that they had also been providing finance, weapons and technology to assist the Montenegrins in the construction of a fortress on the remote peak of the Lovcen, overlooking and threatening the Austrian naval base of Cattaro.[30]

Triple Alliance goodwill foundered on the rocks of the Lovcen. There was no way in which it could be salvaged. San Giuliano could have no reply to Austrian accusations of bad faith, and Germany intervened again in an attempt to moderate the tensions between its two allies. The Germans had cause to be concerned: nothing could have been more utterly embarassing for Berlin than a war between its only two allies, in an area and at a time when one could expect the Russians to intervene, and also possibly the French. But once again there was no showdown. The Austrians were incapable of bringing themselves to face the implications of war with Italy in the Balkans, and the Italians were still in no shape to fight anybody. The war of 1912–13 had, in many ways, been immensely rewarding for them. They had increased the population of their Empire by 60 per cent, and its size by 230 per cent;* they had developed a new technology of war; and they had sustained a naval offensive which had carried the tricolour triumphantly from Bizerta to Assab. But their participation in the struggle for the Mediterranean did have certain drawbacks. In the first place, it had proved far more long-drawn-out and consequently expensive than the Italians had estimated – it was likely to be years before Italy would be in a fit economic condition to fight a major war again. And this situation was made the more serious by the fact that the war of 1911–12 had done more than any other diplomatic initiative over the past century to make a European war of incalculable dimensions a genuinely imminent prospect. By destroying the last elements of Turkish control in the Balkans it had unleashed the untameable nationalism and feelings there; and it had provided the stimulus for an Anglo-French naval accord which, at the very least, guaranteed that Britain would not be able to support Germany in any confrontation between that country and France, and would in practice make it very difficult for the British not actively to support France.

All this was made far more dangerous by the fact that the war of 1911–12 had helped to land the Italians in a diplomatic position which left them the absolute minimum of flexibility. San Giuliano had chosen to believe that tensions between France and Italy compelled his country to work strictly within the framework of the Triple Alliance. But tensions between Italy and Austria made this impossible. The result was not quite isolation: Italy could always go into the diplomatic marketplace and bargain for its security. But it had nothing left to do now but bargain.

The only consolation now for San Giuliano was that Italy had plenty to bargain with. There was no doubt any longer

* The provinces annexed by Italy under the terms of the Treaty of Ouchy had an area of 406,000 square miles, and a population of about 523,176. *Statesman's Yearbook*, 1916

about the position of the Kingdom in the European hierarchy. It was a Great Power in population, wealth and military capacity. It had, in 1914, a population of 35 millions, only four millions less than that of France itself; a national income three and one half times that of the next-ranking European state, Spain;[31] and the fourth navy and the fifth army in Europe. Its economic position was improving impressively. Italian industrial production increased by 83 per cent between 1900 and 1913, while Austrian output increased by only 50 per cent.[32] Expansion in the basic industries was even more remarkable. Italian coal production had gone up by 84 per cent, iron by 220 per cent and steel by 660 per cent in the same period,[33] compared to which Austrian figures were only 20 per cent, 33 per cent and 120 per cent. But the Italian achievement was still impressive only in relative terms: electrical output was the one resource of the Kingdom which really compared with those of the other Great Powers.[34] In 1914 Italy still produced only 781,000 tons of coal, 706,000 tons of iron and 911,000 tons of steel, whereas Austria produced 47 million tons, 2 million tons and 2.7 million tons respectively. The military importance of the Powers in the European hierarchy had virtually been reversed over the past twenty-five years. In 1890 Italian expenditure on arms had amounted to 9.6 per cent of the total arms expenditure of the European Great Powers, while Austrian expenditure had constituted only 7.2 per cent. The respective figures at the beginning of 1914 were 7.1 and 9.0 per cent. Austrian outlays on arms had more than doubled between 1910 and 1914, rising from £17.4 million to £36.4 million, and its naval budget had almost tripled in this time, from £2.8 million to £7.6 million. Italian expenditure on arms increased meanwhile by only 25 per cent, from £24.4 million to £28.2 million. Austria was outspending Italy on defence in 1914 for the first time in twenty-five years.

But this was not a race which the Austrians could reasonably expect to win. The Habsburg Empire could still command greater economic resources than the Kingdom of Italy: the national incomes of the two Powers in 1914 have been estimated at about £1,100 million and £800 million respectively.[35] But Italy's income per head was already higher, at an estimated level of £23 compared with £21; its rate of economic expansion was far higher; and there was no doubt that the Italians would increasingly be able to afford a level of arms expenditure higher, both relatively and absolutely, than the Empire could bear.* There was thus every reason to suspect that Italy would inevitably displace Austria from its present position as fifth among the European Great Powers.

By March 1914 the French had already concluded that Italy was leading the Triple Alliance. And although this was hardly true in the positive sense – the Consulta was certainly not inspiring policy decisions consciously in Berlin or Vienna – there was no doubt that the Germans at least were sufficiently convinced by now of the importance of keeping Italy in the Alliance and that they were committed to a policy of conciliating Italian ambitions in the Balkans and the Mediterranean. The Austrians for their part could hardly oppose the Italians effectively without German support. Nor was there any doubt that the German concern was justified. It was not merely that Italy would soon become a stronger and richer ally than the Habsburg Empire, but in terms of the calculations of 1914 Italy already had the power either to guarantee victory for Germany and Austria in a war against the Franco-Russian alliance, or to render their defeat certain if it fought against them. This seemed inevitable whether the war was long or short. Italian economic capacity would certainly seem to be decisive in a long war. The combined national incomes of the German and Austrian Empires amounted to about £3,150 millions, compared with an estimated £2,650 millions for France and Russia, the Central Powers would thus

* Taylor gives figures for the percentage of national income devoted to armaments in 1914 as 6·1 per cent for Austria and 3·5 per cent for Italy (*Struggle for Mastery*, p. xxix). Stamp's estimates would give comparative figures of about 3·4 per cent each. This discrepancy does not affect the real argument here, which is simply that the Italians could afford to spend more on arms than could the Austrians

have seemed not to need Italy's support in a long war. But the positions of comparative strength would be almost exactly reversed if the Italians were to throw in their hand with Paris and St Petersburg. And Italian support would be absolutely essential on this calculation for the Central Powers, if the British National Income of £2,250 millions were added to that of Russia and France. It is true, however, that as nobody in Europe was really counting on a long war, estimates of varying economic strength were not considered the most relevant. But the position of Italy seemed even more crucial in the case of the short war that was actually anticipated. Conrad von Hotzendorf estimated that the Triple Alliance would be able to deploy 160 divisions for immediate action against the 211 divisions of Russia, France, Serbia, Montenegro and Romania, making the odds against the Alliance 5 to 4. But these manageable odds would become 5 to 3 if Italy remained neutral, and would reach the quite unacceptable level of 2 to 1 if Italy's estimated thirty-four divisions were to be aligned with the enemies of the Central Powers.[36] The weakest of the Great Powers held the balance in Europe.

None of this made life any easier at the Consulta in the spring of 1914. All the potential bargaining power in the world did not alter the fact that relations between Italy and the Habsburg Empire seemed beyond hope of improvement. Nor was Italy in a position to seek an active solution. The armed services were still in desperate need of reorganization and re-equipment after the war for the Mediterranean; diplomatic flexibility had been reduced almost to nothing by San Giuliano's decision to opt exclusively for the Triple Alliance; and Prime Minister Antonio Salandra was far too concerned with coping with incipient revolution in the Romagna to help San Giuliano solve the problems he had created for himself. Meanwhile, the situation deteriorated still further. The tide of Italian economic penetration reached the Turkish littoral, where Italian enterprise began to establish itself in the old Roman province of Adalia. Then in June 1914 the Italian government suggested that William of Wied should abandon the Albanian throne, which he hardly seemed competent to occupy. The Austrians flatly refused. And their attitude could only become even more intransigent. Franz Joseph could not be expected to live much longer, also his heir apparent, Franz Ferdinand, was a man who combined most of the more aggressively objectionable qualities available to a human being,* with great intelligence, unremitting energy, contempt for Italy, ambitions for Salonika and a determination to solve the internal and foreign problems of the Habsburg Empire by elevating its Slav subject peoples into some kind of a master-race category, in a Tripartite Imperial Federation.

No prospect could have been less welcome to the Italians. It was not part of their policy to foster the nationalistic ambitions of the Balkan peoples. Their mission was rather to supplant the Austrians as the predominant exploiting power in south-eastern Europe. Italy's bid for greatness in this direction would be jeopardized in the most serious manner possible if the Habsburg Empire could somehow achieve a reconciliation with its Slav subject peoples.

There were, however, two reasons for hoping that this might not happen. The first was that such a reconciliation was not desired by Serbia, the independent Slav state most assiduously fostering disaffection within the Habsburg Empire. Belgrade had its own concept of imperialism, which involved in its more restrained moments domination over all the various peoples from the Danube to the Aegean, and Franz Ferdinand's unfortunate combination of obstinacy and detestability ensured that he would be prepared to take risks which would daunt other men, and that few people would be likely to try to dissuade him from taking them.

Such a risk was his decision to visit the Bosnian capital of Sarajevo in his capacity as Inspector-General of the Imperial Forces, 'on St Vitus's day, the 525th anniversary of the Serbian

* Salandra lists his chief qualities as 'harsh, avaricious, autocratic, bigoted and inclined to look down on subject peoples'. (Antonio Salandra, *op. cit.*, p. 20.) Albertini suggests that he was probably also insane

3a. First World War Caproni bomber

Imperial War Museum

3b. Torpedo-bomber, Savoja-Marchetti SM 79-II

Imperial War Museum

4a. First World War: Italian motor convoy in the mountains
Radio Times Hulton Picture Library

4b. Second World War: MAS boat preparing to put to sea, surrounded by a fleet of minesweepers *Imperial War Museum*

defeat at Kosovo in 1389, which for the first time was to be solemnly celebrated now that in 1912 the defeat had been wiped out at Kumanovo'.[37] Taylor suggests appropriately that such a visit to such a place at such a time was equivalent to having the Prince of Wales visit Dublin on St Patrick's Day at the height of the Troubles.[38] The weirdness of the misjudgment involved was made the more striking by certain premonitions of disaster which Ferdinand claimed to have had. No man in history was ever more entitled to them. But the news of his assassination on 28 June 1914 evoked sentiments of positive relief in Italy. The man who had publicly resolved to take Salonika[39] and to fight Italy[40] had been fortuitously removed from the scene. San Giuliano relayed the news to Salandra in an unbelievably flippant telephone conversation.[41] Crowds in Rome hailed the news with cheers and patriotic songs, and the mood of relief continued in Italy until the presentation of the Austrian ultimatum to Serbia on 23 July, nearly a month later. This was not to say that the Italians were without their worries. Nobody really expected that the death of Franz Ferdinand would resolve all the tensions between Vienna and Rome. Bollati, the Italian Ambassador in Berlin, sent San Giuliano a brilliant summary on 8 July, depicting with complete accuracy the hopeless state of relations between the Triple Alliance partners:

> 'It is impossible to imagine a stranger or more dangerous situation. . . . If there were nothing more than the Albanian question dividing us! But there are so many other causes of dissension . . . the Lovcen question, the possible conflict between Austria and Serbia, the awful problem of a possible union between Serbia and Montenegro . . . the possession by Austria of provinces of Italian race and tongue which, in the consciousness of, to say the least, nine-tenths of the Italians of the Kingdom, belong *de jure* to Italy and must one day or another belong to her also *de facto*; the treatment by Austria of the populations of those provinces; the clerical question; the failure to return our Sovereign's visit . . . in such condi-

tions the slightest incident is sufficient to cause complications and jeopardise the stability of the alliance.

In reality there is not one single question in which the interests of Italy are not, or are not thought to be, in conflict with those of Austria. . . .'[42]

Bollati had of course left out the most important point of conflict – but this was because he was not yet aware of it. His analysis was in any case an immensely grave indictment of San Giuliano's foreign policy. No principles of action which had committed Italy to such an alliance could possibly be the right ones. But San Giuliano had done more than this. His dedicated pursuit of conciliation towards Vienna had led the German and Austrian leadership to assume that Italy's adherence to the Triple Alliance could be counted on, in any circumstances. It was a conclusion which admittedly could have recommended itself only to minds second-rate, frivolously uninformed, or wilfully closed to reality. Such minds were as it happened determining policy in Berlin and Vienna.

Kaiser Wilhelm had no doubt as to the appropriate response for the Austrians to make to the Sarajevo assassination: his comment on 30 June was that the Serbs would have to be disposed of. It was certainly manifest that Austria would never have a better chance of doing just that, with the general approval, or at least toleration, of most of Europe. The German Ambassador, in conveying this reaction to Berchtold on 2 July, added the warning that the Italians would have to be told, in order to preserve the unity of the Alliance.[43] This view was supported by Conrad, who had done his calculations, arrived at the estimates already mentioned (see page 63) and concluded that the country against which he had wanted to make war for the past six years was also an indispensable ally of the Habsburg Empire. Berchtold rejected the idea of consultations with Italy, however, on the grounds that the Italians would demand Valona in Albania as compensation if Austria attempted to extend its territories in the Balkans. His resolve was strengthened by a communication from German Chancellor Bethmann-Hollwegg on 6 July, urging that Austria, while doing nothing to jeopardize relations with Italy, take immediate action against the Serbs, but without necessarily entering into discussions with the Italians.

Bethmann-Hollwegg might have been expected to understand that there was no move that the Austrians could take against Serbia which would not alarm the Italians, and that there was nothing in the meantime that could alarm them more seriously than the fact that they were not being told what the Austrians had in mind. Such approaches as they received from the Habsburg Empire only made things worse. San Giuliano, physically tortured by the gout and arthritis which were about to kill him, and mentally anguished by the shipwreck of his policy, was approached on 10 July by German Ambassador Hans von Flotow with the suggestion that Austria might be prepared to accept a union between Serbia and Montenegro, if it were to receive the Lovcen as compensation. San Giuliano distractedly replied that a move against the Lovcen would mean war between Austria and Italy. However, he then attempted to salvage something from the wreck of Austro-Italian relations by suggesting that Italy might regard the return of the Trentino as an adequate exchange for the Lovcen.

Whereas Flotow's proposal indicated sufficiently the total failure of Berlin to comprehend the nature of the conflicting imperial rivalries in the Balkans, San Giuliano's reference to the Trentino was enough for its part to convince such uncomprehending minds that Italy would condone an assault on Serbia if it offered a sufficiently attractive bribe. This was exactly the opposite impression from that which had been unequivocally conveyed to Vienna in July 1913. But at that time San Giuliano had been backed by the Germans. Now he was sure that the Germans were backing Austria.

San Giuliano's alarm continued to grow. By 15 July he was convinced that the Austrians had decided on aggressive action in the Balkans. By the 16th he was convinced that war was inevitable. Meanwhile, German Foreign Minister Gottlieb von

Jagow had given support to Tschirschky's original recommendation that Italy be kept in the Triple Alliance. Flotow's report of his conversation with San Giuliano even inspired him to suggest to Berchtold on 15 July that Italy should be given the Trentino, in recognition of its right to compensation under the terms of the Agreement of December 1909, if Austria were to alter the *status quo* in the Balkans. But this was almost as unrealistic as suggesting that Italy should let Austria have the Lovcen. On 20 July Berchtold again rejected the idea of offering the Italians compensation. He could of course still hope that the mere fact that San Giuliano had raised the possibility of a deal indicated that Italy was still interested in remaining with the Alliance. Nothing less could have satisfied his military advisers. Conrad said flatly on 23 July: 'If we have to fear Italy as well, then let us not mobilise.'[44] Bethmann-Hollwegg told Tschirschky on 26 July that von Moltke also was adamant that Italian support was essential, and that reasonable compensation would have to be offered to Italy to keep it in the Alliance.

San Giuliano could have stopped the movement towards war dead in its tracks any time before 29 July. All that was required was an unequivocal statement that Italy would regard itself as released from its obligations under the terms of the Triple Alliance if Austria were to take aggressive action against Serbia. A clear invitation to do so had been made by the Russians. Sazonov's appeal, conveyed to San Giuliano on 27 July, suggested that Italy 'could play an outstanding part in the preservation of peace if she would exercise suitable influence on Austria, and adopt a definitely disapproving attitude towards the conflict . . .'.[45] But San Giuliano was incapable of acting on this advice. It had after all been his only policy to seek to identify Italian interests as closely as possible with those of the Habsburg Empire, and his dedication to this approach had left him with no alternative to restort to if things went wrong. Neither was it easy to see what Italy would have gained by checking Vienna's lurch into war in this manner. The Triple Alliance would have been broken; declared enmity would have existed between Italy and Austria; and any hope of compensation in the Balkans or the Trentino would necessarily have been lost. On the credit side, eleven million lives would have been saved; but San Giuliano was not to have known this.

What he had already done instead was to recommend that the government in Belgrade simply yield to the Austrians' demands, in the hope that wiser counsels might eventually prevail, which would still have been preferable to a world war. But San Giuliano had left it too late, until after the Serbs had already declined to accede to certain points of the Austrian ultimatum. He then dashed off a letter to German Ambassador Merey on 28 July, assuring him that the Italian government, 'animated by the friendly feelings towards Austria-Hungary, has made and will continue to make every effort to persuade Serbia to accept the demands contained in the Imperial and Royal Government's note of 24 July 1914 . . .'. However, he then pointed out that it

> '. . . was on the basis of Article VII [of the Triple Alliance] and of the agreements on the Sanjak of Novi-bazar and on Albania that the cordial collaboration of Italian and Austro-Hungarian displomacy must be founded . . . agreement on this point is urgent, for so long as it has not been arrived at and doubt can subsist as to the interpretation given by Austria-Hungary to Article VII, Italy cannot pursue a policy which would now or later facilitate occupations by Austria-Hungary, whether temporary or permanent, and must, on the contrary, favour whatever would lessen the probability of such occupations, while, however, endeavouring as far as possible to reconcile this line of conduct, imposed by the need for safeguarding her vital interests, with her keen desire to render more and more intimate the relations between the two Allied Powers, which have made so much progress in recent years and may well make further progress on a basis of the harmony and conciliation of mutual relations. . . .'

Albertini comments that this Note makes painful reading.[46]

It is certainly among the most supine of diplomatic missives. The only progress that Austro-Italian relations had made during the past eighteen months was to bring both countries to the verge of breaking relations entirely. Nothing could have sounded less like a call to Vienna to halt. Its only coherent message was a plea for compensation, which was by now nothing but a forlorn hope. Berchtold was already describing Italy's attitude as that of Shylock with his pound of flesh.[47] His reply of 28 July maintained that, as Austria had no territorial acquisitions in mind, the question of compensation did not arise. There could never be any question in any case of 'detaching any portion of the Monarchy', and Italy was never to have hopes of the Trentino. All that was offered was a promise of an exchange of views if Austria were to enter upon permanent occupation of Serb territory. In return, 'we expect of Italy that the Kingdom will not impede its ally in the action necessary to the attainment of its ends, and will steadily maintain the foreshadowed friendly attitude towards us in accordance with the Treaty'.[48]

This was totally unsatisfactory. San Giuliano's policy had made shipwreck in two ways. The Austrians had never been interested in compensating Italy to stay neutral: the only thing that could have shaken their position was an unequivocal warning that Italy would positively oppose an uncompensated Austrian move in the Balkans, and this San Giuliano was incapable of presenting. However, the fact was that Italy could not tolerate any increase of Austrian power in the Balkans which was not compensated for by a corresponding increase of Italian authority. The positions of Rome and Vienna were in fact incompatible.

All that was needed was someone with the courage to tell this to Italy's Triple Alliance partners, a quality so much lacking among the Italian diplomats that they were actively trying to avoid the company of the German and Austrian colleagues. Meanwhile, Europe rolled on into war. Austria declared war on Serbia on 28 July. Two days later San Giuliano was still managing to convey the impression to German Ambassador Flotow that Italy was not bound to take part in a world war resulting from Austrian aggression against Serbia. But he reiterated that he was not saying that Italy would not take part in the end: he was merely registering that it was not bound to fight.[49] This could only be intended to hold out the hope that Italy might yet be induced positively to assist its Triple Alliance partners in war. The result was that Berchtold still believed as late as 31 July that Italy could actually be persuaded to enter into war with Russia and France, while on the same day Italian Chief of Staff Luigi Cadorna was still pondering over the best means of sending an Italian expeditionary force to Germany. But that morning his proposals were rendered nugatory by a meeting of the Italian Cabinet. There had never indeed been a choice, rationally speaking. No Italian government could have brought the kingdom into a war to fight for Habsburg domination of the Balkans, and the defeat of Italian designs on the region. Not only gradually was the decision for neutrality broken to the world outside. It emerged initially as an unofficial press report on the morning of 1 August, before Germany had actually declared war on Russia. A further statement on the following morning announced that 'certain European Powers are in a state of war and . . . Italy is at peace with all the belligerents. . . .' The royal assent to the decision for neutrality was not sought until 2 August, however, and not conveyed officially to Berlin and Vienna until 3 August. Even then, Ambassador Bollati in Berlin sent the Italian Note by messenger, claiming that he was too indisposed to see Jagow in person.

The Italians had done all that they could, reasonably speaking. They could not in all fairness assist the Austrians in the Balkans and they were still too weak to challenge them directly. But their declaration of neutrality was in itself an act of defiance. San Giuliano tried to appease Vienna and Berlin with long protestations of Italian goodwill and explanations of the practical considerations dissuading Italy from going to war just then. But these were totally without effect in the capitals of Italy's erstwhile allies. Wilhelm II denounced Victor Emmanuel as a scoundrel and San Giuliano as an insolent liar; Berchtold categorized the Italian policy as 'blackmailing'; and von Moltke reassured Conrad that: 'Italy's felony will avenge itself in future history. God give you victory now that you may later settle accounts with those scoundrels.'[50]

For the simple fact was that all that Italy could hope for now was the military defeat of its Alliance partners. Victory for the Central Powers would mean at the very best the loss of all Italy's territorial ambitions in south-eastern Europe; it would also very probably mean the military subjugation of Italy. German military leaders accepted that the Austro-Serbian war would in all likelihood be followed by an Austro-Italian War – which of course did not mean that Italy was committed to siding with the Entente. It could conceivably be advantageous to come to the rescue of its foundering Alliance partners. But there were two factors which made this option improbable. One was the problem of making sure that Germany and Austria would pay their debts after a victory owed to Italian intervention; the other was that it was unlikely that Austria would be able to offer what Italy really wanted, even *in extremis*: it would be easier for governments in London, Paris and St Petersburg than for the Imperial and royal government in Vienna to give away parts of the Habsburg Empire.

Bargaining began immediately. The Italian Ambassador in St Petersburg suggested to the Russians on 1 August the conditions under which Italy might be induced to side with the Entente. Sazonov agreed heartily that Italy should be rewarded with Valona and the Trentino.[51] These terms were endorsed on 5 August by French Foreign Minister Domergue. British Foreign Minister Grey added Trieste to the list, then on 7 August Sazonov raised the bid to embrace supremacy in the Adriatic, as well as Trieste, Valona and the Trentino. Salandra also proposed to the British that Italy should in addition receive the Mediterranean provinces of Turkey, on the assumption that the territorial integrity of the Ottoman Empire was not in any case going to be preserved. The vision of a great Italian Empire was rising in the east.

This was exactly what was beginning to disturb the leaders of the Entente. Neither France nor Russia wanted to see Italy established in the Balkans and the Levant as a far more formidable and rapacious successor to the Habsburg Empire. Neither were they willing to concede to demands in a way which would enable the Italians to screw a still higher price out of Germany and Austria. Most important, however, was the fact that it was becoming increasingly obvious that the Entente could survive without the help of Italy. The German advance was admittedly still continuing in France; but so was the Russian advance against Germany, in East Prussia. On 16 August the long-delayed Austrian assault on Belgrade was hurled back in defeat on the Jadar river and on the following day the Russians parried and threw back a wild German counter-offensive in East Prussia, at Stalluponen. This tide of Slav victory impelled Sazonov to remind Paris and London that Serbia would need an outlet to the sea, so that Italy would not be able to demand the Dalmatian coast south of Ragusa. However, the Russian advance against Germany was disastrously checked at Tannenberg the following week, although this setback was seemingly compensated for by a victory of greater magnitude won by the Russians in Galicia, against the hopelessly confused troops of Conrad von Hotzendorf. Fortunes see-sawed dizzily in September. The Germans fell back from the Marne; the Russians won more victories in Galicia and suffered more crushing defeats in East Prussia; and the Serbs and Montenegrins triumphantly invaded the Habsburg province of Bosnia. Then the Central Powers rallied under German direction, forced the Western Allies to abandon Antwerp, and began doggedly forcing the Russians back along the whole eastern front, towards Warsaw and the San. Then once again the German counter-attack in the West was checked at Ypres, and in a magnificent campaign the Russians rallied to drive the Germans and Austrians all the way back to their starting line, renewing their incursions into the sacred territory of East Prussia.

This gave the Italians an opportunity to safeguard their own interests in the Balkans. The Greeks had sought to capitalize on the preoccupations of the Great Powers by renewing their own demands on the northern Epirus as soon as Italian-sponsored rebels under Essed Pasha had driven the hapless William of Wied from Albania. The next few weeks hardly seemed propitious for an Italian intervention. Salandra watched impotently while the Greeks established a puppet government of the 'Autonomous Epirus', seized Korachia, and set out to destroy and massacre the people of 300 villages in the Argyrocastro Province.[52] Meanwhile, things had changed at the Consulta. San Guiliano had died, and to his successor, the remote, scholarly, and appropriately uncompromising Baron Sidney Sonnino, a hard-line policy seemed both safe and congenial. On 29 October, Salandra landed what was inspiringly called a 'sanitary mission' at Valona, to protect the inhabitants and deter the Greeks,[53] and on the following day, Admiral Patris landed a further 200 marines to secure the strategically situated island of Sasen, at the mouth of Valona harbour. For a moment it looked as if the Italians might have overplayed their hand. The Austrian armies mounted yet another offensive against the Slav states, occupying Belgrade on 2 December, only to be ousted again on 3 December, when the Serbs and Montenegrins went over to the offensive all along the line. Meanwhile, the Russians and Germans clashed in their most extensive encounter yet, at Lodz, eighty miles south-west of Warsaw, when the Grand Duke Nicholas' plans for a winter offensive, which might have been the greatest of Russian victories, ended in bitterly-conceded defeat. But this was essentially a defensive victory: the Austrians still lay broken and inert in the South; and the prospect of an early victory for either camp seemed more remote than ever.

It seemed a good time for a powerful neutral to drive a bargain. Salandra and Sonnino opened exploratory talks with the Austrians on 28 January 1915. But Vienna held to the fatuous position that compensation should be paid by Italy to the Habsburg Empire, in view of the continued Italian occupation of the Dodecanese.[54] The German position was still unchanged: any reasonable cession should be made which would preserve Italian goodwill, and this included the Trentino, at least up to the linguistic frontier. But the Austrians had an answer for this too: they proposed that the Germans secure peace in the West by ceding Alsace-Lorraine to France. Meanwhile, another bid by Germany for a quick victory in the East failed on the Nieman, in the Winter Battle of Masuria. It was the familiar experience: the German attack was substantially successful, the supporting Austrian one a total failure, and the envisaged decisive encirclement accordingly incomplete. The Russians had been driven from East Prussia again but they were still resolutely in the war.

Sazonov seemed to find this result positively encouraging. On 3 March he renewed his opposition to Italian encroachments along the Adriatic littoral, arguing that Italian intervention had lost its value by now anyway. For a moment it seemed as if the only advocate of concessions among the belligerents was Conrad von Hotzendorf, who had no delusions about the condition of Austria's armed forces, and was prepared to give the Italians anything they wanted in the meantime, including the Trentino, on the grounds that territory ceded now could be always recovered after victory.

But time was on the Italians' side. The French had lost faith in the offensive at last, after losing 90,000 casualties in the Winter Battle of Champagne, without any compensating gains. The British began with better fortune at Neuve-Chapelle, on 10 March, but lost almost all their gains when the Germans counter-attacked. Salandra accordingly raised his price. What he now demanded was the Trentino; Istria; the Dalmatian coast as far south as the River Neretva, midway between Spalato and Cattaro; Saseno and Valona in Albania, along with the northern Epirus hinterland; and the establishment of Durazzo and its hinterland as an allegedly autonomous Moslem state in central Albania. At this point, however, the fall of the great Austrian fortress of Prezemysl on 22 March helped to strengthen Russian opposition. The Entente ministers demanded that Italy's southern expansion in Dalmatia should be halted at Cape Planka, ninety-five miles north of the Neretva, whereupon Sonnino presented another set of demands to Vienna, involving substantially the same concessions as those sought from the Entente, with the addition of a pledge to end Austrian intervention in Albania. He received his reply on 17 April, conceding a greater area of the Trentino, but making no reference to the Balkan territories. Salandra's response to this was to press, with renewed energy, negotiations with the Entente. On 26 April the Treaty of London was signed, conceding Italy the Tyrol as far as the Brenner; Gorizia, Trieste and the Julian Alps as far as Fiume; Istria, the Dalmatian coast between Zara and Spalato, and the offshore islands as far south as Ragusa; but reserving Fiume in the north to be handed over as a port to the proposed new state of Croatia.

Details were never made public until released by the Bolsheviks, after their capture of Petrograd. It was not the happiest of arrangements. Sazonov had called the cession of even eighty miles of the Dalmatian coast a challenge to the Slav conscience; Delcasse was reported to have said that Italy had held a pistol to the head of the Entente; and Slav agents, having discovered some of the terms of the Treaty, reported them back to their peoples, with the result that Slavs in the Austrian army prepared to fight vigorously on behalf of their present oppressors, against their proposed new ones. But the Italians had even more serious problems. On 4 May, just when the Treaty of the Triple Alliance was being denounced in Rome the roar of 950 German and Austrian cannons announced the achievement of a breakthrough between Gorlice and Tarnow. In ten days, the Russians had been driven back 80 miles, and the greatest of Austro-German victories had been won. Meanwhile, the best-planned of French offensives, driven home by the best troops in the French army, foundered in Artois, with no gains and 100,000 casualties. And in Abyssinia, the Negus Micail was massing 150,000 warriors on Italy's frontier in Eritrea, which would be impossible to defend. Rome had backed the losing side.

3 : To Win a War

ITALY had not of course had much choice. Only the Entente had been prepared to offer the concessions that would secure Italian interests in the Adriatic; and only the Entente could be trusted even partially to make its offers good. Salandra's decision of 5 May was the logical culmination of thirty-three years of Italian foreign policy. Italian manipulation of Great Power rivalries had prepared the way for Italian aggression in North Africa that would involve the breakdown of Turkish authority in the Balkans; Italian intrigues at Cetinje for an easy escape from the consequences of North African aggression had resulted in nationalism in the Balkans which had given rise to such intense feelings that it had converted south-eastern Europe into an arena for Great Power conflict. Italian equivocations when such a conflict developed had encouraged the Central Powers to press on with designs on Serbian independence which led to world conflict. In other words, it was Italy's war and now the Italians were in it. They were also going to pay for their actions more dearly than any other member of the Entente. But at least they knew what they were fighting for, and that was the replacement of Austria by themselves as the dominant force in south-eastern Europe. All they had to do was win.

It was the supreme challenge of Italy's history as a nation, but that was not to say the nation was in a fit condition to meet it. General Luigi Cadorna, Chief of the Italian General Staff since July 1914, had managed to raise the available strength of the army in that time from about 300,000 men to 875,000,[1] and the field artillery was comparable in numbers and quality with those of the enemy. An Italian division of twelve battalions was supported by thirty-two guns, the same as were available for a similar number of Austrian battalions*, compared with a French division's complement of thirty-four guns and a German's of seventy-two. But light, quick-firing field guns were of little effect against entrenchments, which could be destroyed economically only by big guns firing high-explosive shells with a deep trajectory, with which the Italians were poorly equipped, while the Austrians produced in their Skoda works large numbers of the biggest and best howitzers in the world. Moreover, an Italian division was equipped with only eight machine-guns at the start of the war, while the French, Germans and Austrians alike could deploy twenty-four of these vital defensive weapons for a comparable number of battalions.[2] The Italians would thus face the gravest difficulties, whether they attacked or remained on the defensive. Nor was their position even at sea entirely satisfactory. The Italian fleet was certainly bigger and better that the Habsburg navy: Admiral Thaon di Revel could deploy in the Adriatic eight battleships with a total displacement of 119,000 tons against the Austrians' seven capital ships of 70,000 tons; sixteen cruisers against their three; forty-eight destroyers against their eighteen; and eighty-one torpedo-boats against their sixty-six. The Austrians were numerically stronger only in submarines, of which they had twenty-seven against the Italians' nineteen.[3] But they had immensely more advantageous bases. Pola was less than 100 miles from Venice, while the Italian main fleet was stationed 425 miles away, at Brindisi.[4] There was thus every likelihood that the Austrians would be able to dominate the Adriatic by their ability to concentrate force far more rapidly than the Italians. The experience of Lissa suggested that they might not have much to fear from Italian maritime grand strategy.

Italy should have had the advantage that it could throw virtually its whole strength against Austria, while Austria had

* An Austrian division consisted of fifteen battalions, the Italian, French, and German divisions of twelve battalions each

perforce to divide its fighting capacity among three fronts. But much of this potential benefit had already been lost, thanks to the delay in mobilizing the Italian army, as a result of Sazonov's indefatigable opposition to offering Italy terms which would make it worth its while to enter the war at all.[5] After the outbreak of hostilities on 1 August 1914, Conrad had retained only five divisions on the Italian front.[6] He had transferred another three there by April 1915. The enormous deliverance of Gorlice made it possible for him to detach from the Russian front the equivalent of four more complete divisions. The Austrians had also been able to construct artillery emplacements and concealed pillboxes, to strengthen the most formidable natural defences in Europe.[7] The front ran for about 480 miles. Its first section, the Trentino, consisted of almost impregnable mountain buttresses, divided on the west by the most precipitous carriage pass in the Alps, more than 9,000 feet above sea level, and on the east by defiles practically useless for a modern invader. The second part of the front was sheer mountain rampart, and the third, the Isonzo, the most militarily defensible river barrier in Europe.

The prospect that faced Cadorna in May 1915 could hardly be called inviting. And his hopes could scarcely have been raised by a startling demonstration of Austrian readiness and enthusiasm for war. In the hours following Italy's challenge, two battleships, four cruisers and an escorting screen of destroyers and torpedo-boats swept out of Pola under an umbrella of Austrian aircraft, and assailed the eastern Italian seaboard for 320 miles, from Venice to Manfredonia. Venice itself was bombed from the air, railway stations were shelled along the whole length of the coastline, an Italian torpedo-boat base at Porto Corsini was bombarded, and an Italian destroyer was damaged off Manfredonia. The raiders all returned to base safely. The worst memories of Lissa had been revived. Italian concern over the strategic dangers of the Adriatic littoral had been shown to be fully justified.

This first raid of the Habsburg navy was none the less almost the last – only once again, in February 1916, was Italian command of the Adriatic challenged. Nor did it have any discouraging effect upon Cadorna. Efficient and untiring, as well as doctrinaire, domineering, narrow-minded, unfeeling and rude, he was the last of men to be swayed by circumstances. He had in fact already ordered an immediate offensive by the second and third armies against the Isonzo positions, while the fourth and fifth armies attacked in the Trentino, to prevent the Austrians from shifting reserves. About thirty-five divisions were immediately available. Meanwhile, Italian destroyers sailed into the Gulf of Trieste to shell the railway and shipyards at Monfalcone, which were also attacked by Italian bombers. This was followed on 30 May by another air raid, on Pola, and by 16 June the preliminary offensives on the Isonzo and in the Trentino were over. The Italians had advanced, at the cost of extremely heavy casualties, as much as fifteen miles in the East, and ten in the West. It was to take them three-and-a-half years and 650,000 lives to cover the next five miles across Isonzo.

With the British attempt at an outflanking move on the Gallipoli Peninsula going down in defeat before the heights of Helles; the Germans attacking again in France, in the Argonne; and on 22 June the Russians abandoning Lemberg, the capital of Galicia and their greatest prize of the war, the situation once more began to look serious. Realizing the need for prompt action on the part of the Allies, Cadorna did not delay long in making his second effort. After barely a week's respite, his troops were sent on 23 June to make the first assault on the Isonzo positions. Then when almost no gains were achieved in a fortnight's unremitting fighting, he halted on 7 July to bring more urgently needed heavy artillery, and on 18 July launched a second assault, which was sustained for sixteen days. The fighting was fiercer, the casualties still heavier, and even less territory conquered. Cadorna paused again, this time for more than two months; brought up still more artillery and reserves; and began all over again on 18 October.

This time he had a new card to play. Although Italy had been the first belligerent nation to explore actively the possibilities of attack from the air, not only had it entered the world conflict weaker in aviation than any other of the major combatants, but whatever strength it did have in this regard had actually deteriorated during the months of neutrality. In 1914 the combined Italian air services could have deployed fifty-eight aircraft against a total Austrian strength of fifty. But by March 1915 the Austrians had accumulated twenty-four seaplanes and ninety-six landplanes, against an Italian total of fifteen and ninety respectively. However, the inspiration of Douhet and the valour of Piazza and Gavotti had not been without result. In 1915 only Italy and Russia could deploy genuine bombing planes, designed specifically for use as a strategic bombardment force. The Russians had led the way with Igor Ivanovich Sikorsky's *Russkii Vitiaz* of May 1913, which was the first four-engined aircraft in the world. This was succeeded by the *Ilya Muromets,* which entered service in 1914 as the world's first multi-engined heavy bomber possessed by an air force.[8] By 1915 about twenty aircraft of this class were on combat duty. Meanwhile, in 1913, the Italian firm of Caproni had also developed a multi-engined aircraft, the Ca30, powered by three engines. This was modified in 1915 as the Ca32, carrying the same weight of bombs as the *Ilya Muromets* (about 1,250 pounds) but higher, further and faster than the huge Russian aircraft. With eight of these formidable new bombers providing air support for Cadorna's divisions, a genuine strategic bombing force was being used for the first time in actual combat. Italy was leading the world in air warfare again.

The trim Capronis had made history – but they had not altered the combat situation on the Isonzo. Cadorna's third offensive ground to a halt on 4 November, without having made the slightest impression on the Austrian defences. Cadorna waited for a week, and went over to the offensive again, as drenching autumn rain gave way to freezing winter cold. And it was not only on the Isonzo that Italy's problems were multiplying: internal strife in Abyssinia had succeeded in averting an attack upon virtually defenceless Eritrea. But in the East the Serb defences had collapsed after a three-pronged attack by the

Austrians, Germans and Bulgarians. It had been expected that the Serbs would withdraw towards the south-east, to link up with the two British and French divisions which had been roosting unproductively in Salonika for the past month, but Bulgarian pressure and their own territorial ambitions led the Serbs to head south-west through Albania. So at the height of the three-week battle of the Fourth Isonzo, Cadorna decided on 24 November to despatch Italian troops to Albania to cover the retreat of the Serbs, and to defend Italy's own interest in that strategic part of the Balkans.[9] Thaon di Revel's battle fleet escorted the convoy of dashing transatlantic liners which carried the first of forty-eight battalions across the Adriatic from Italy on 6 December,[10] and effected the rescue of 156,000 Serbs and 27,000 Austrian prisoners. British and French ships took off 70,000 in all.

This triumph of Italian sea power represented the only really rewarding experience that the Italian people had known since Salandra had presented the nation's challenge to Austria in May. The fighting on the Isonzo had turned into a blood-bath of a duration and horror unmatched on any comparable battle-field in Europe. Casualties for the year amounted to 278,000 Italians and 165,000 Austrians killed, wounded, missing or taken prisoner – the Italian dead alone numbered 66,000 – and not the slightest significant alteration in the position of the opposing armies had been effected in return for all this expenditure of human suffering. No troops on earth had yet been called upon to sacrifice so much effort for so little visible return over so long a period. Division for division, Italy's casualty rate was more than two and a half times that suffered by the other Allied Powers on the Western front. Other countries were also to have this experience in 1916. The results of Italy's intervention, although not at first obvious, were vital. Most important was the fact that it had already occasioned a massive redistribution of Austrian man power. Conrad had, as we have seen, been content to leave five of his total of sixty-six divisions on the Italian frontier in August 1914. By May 1915 he had added to this force a further seven divisions, thereby depriving the Germans of the man power needed fully to exploit the great Gorlice-Tarnow breakthrough; and by the end of 1915, a third of the Austrian army, twenty-two divisions in all, had been committed to the Italian front, thereby critically weakening Austria's none-too-impressive defences in Russia,[11] and compounding the anxieties of the already overstrained Germans. Moreover, Italian industry was also beginning to respond to the challenge of war. Production of machine-guns had quadrupled from twenty-five per month in 1914, to 100 per month in 1915;[12] aircraft production had risen even more impressively, from twelve machines built in the whole of 1914,[13] to 382 in 1915;[14] and already work was beginning on the little ships, the Bersaglieri of the sea, the MAS-boats,* that were to inflict on Austria in the First World War the most completely one-sided naval defeats of the age, and to save the honour of the Italian navy in the Second.

Di Revel's fleet had indeed already demonstrated its command of the Adriatic by the beginning of 1916. Between 27 November 1915 and 4 March 1916 his ships carried from Albania to Corfu 260,895 men, 10,153 horses and sixty-eight cannon;[15] 205,000 of these men were regrouped into a new Serbian army to serve in Greece.[16] The Austrians made only one attempt to interfere with this traffic: on 6 February four destroyers of the Habsburg navy sallied out from their Dalmatian bases, bombarding Ortona and San Vito on the way. They were intercepted by two of di Revel's destroyers on 9 February and driven ignominiously back to Cattaro.

But the demands of a continental war dragged the Italians back into the inferno of the Isonzo. On 21 February Erich von Falkenhayn began a massive assault on Verdun, with the precise

* The initials remained the same, but they came to stand for different things. They meant originally 'Motobarca armata Societa Veneziana Automobile Nautiche'; then 'Motobarca anti-sommergibile' or 'Motobarca armata silurante'; then finally 'Motoscafo anti-sommergibile'. (Aldo Fraccaroli, *Italian Warships of World War I*, Ian Allan, London, 1970, p. 129)

intention, not of capturing the town, but of exhausting French morale and man power in its defence. The French reply was to immediately call on allies for diversionary offensives, and Cadorna was again the first to respond. The Italians were hurled against positions stronger than ever, to fight in the worst possible conditions, until fog, snow and ice brought the offensive to a halt on 29 March. Once more, nothing had been gained.

And indeed so little had been gained for Italy in all these assaults on the Isonzo, that Conrad at last felt he could afford to take the offensive. The Austrian army was moved from the Serbian front to the Trentino, augmented by nine divisions transferred from the Russian front, with 2,000 guns. One immediate effect of this was to infuriate the Germans, who had counted on having some of the Austrian heavy artillery brought from Galicia to assist in the siege of Verdun. They now found to their horror not only that, apart from a few huge Skoda howitzers, the guns were staying where they were, but that they, the Germans, were also expected to find more divisions from their already overstrained resources to replace those transferred by Conrad to the Italian front.[17]

Cadorna at least knew what was coming. Italian air power was already beginning to achieve a dramatic ascendancy over the Habsburg air force. Encounters had been rare and unfruitful in 1915: only two Italian and four Austrian aircraft had been lost in the whole year.[18] But the intensity of the air war multiplied in 1916. On 7 April thirty-four Capronis carried out the biggest bombing attack of the war so far, impelling the Austrians to challenge them in the first real dog-fight over the Italian front.[19] Other scouting flights helped to keep Cardona informed of the Austrian build-up in the Trentino. Preparations to oppose it remained inadequate, however, partly because Cardona's personal unpopularity ensured that none of his subordinate commanders would do what he suggested until he arrived in person to see that his orders were carried out; and partly because the Italian commander on the spot had elected to try to improve his position with local attacks which proved fruitless, rather than settle for a strictly defensive posture which would have been more economical of men and resources.[20] Conrad began his offensive on 10 May. He had no significant numerical advantage over the Italians in terms of man power, but he was able to support his attacks with a huge park of 2,000 guns detached from the Russian front, against the defenders' 850 pieces. His troops continued their advance for twenty-five days across increasingly difficult terrain, under the furious harassment of 279 Italian aircraft. They managed to drive twelve miles deep into the Italian defences. But Conrad's bid for victory in the Asiago had already exposed the Habsburg Empire to perhaps the greatest single disaster in military history.

Cadorna appealed to the Russians for a relieving offensive, as he had himself responded to a French plea after Falkenhayn had begun his assault on Verdun. It was, however, not an expedient time for him to do so. The Russians were already consulting with the Western Allies on the question of how the spoils of the Turkish Empire were to be divided after victory. London and Paris agreed with St Petersburg to divide Anatolia into spheres of influence among the three of them, specifically excluding the Italians. But the Russians could always be counted on to sacrifice their armies in the interests of their allies, they would even sacrifice them for an ally they had just contrived to defraud. The commander of the Russian South-West Army Group, Alexei Brussilov, had had occasion to become familiar with German offensive techniques, when he had been compelled to try to extricate his forces from the Carpathians after the Gorlice-Tarnow breakthrough. He had had the opportunity to observe how the Russian defences had been swamped by a numerically inferior enemy, employing a combination of massed fire power, surprise and recklessly enterprising forward movement. Brussilov's tragically under-gunned divisions would have to count on the last two factors if they were to use the manoeuvre at all. What the Russian commander hoped for was to turn his inability to mount a really adequate covering barrage into a positive advantage, by strengthening the element of surprise. No bombardment that the Russians could deliver would be impressive enough to give clear warning of an impending offensive.

Brussilov's forces began to move forward against the Austrian defences after barely an hour's preliminary barrage. Conrad's subordinates did not even realize that a full-scale Russian offensive was under way, until Brussilov's northern and southern armies advanced against them the following morning. Then the Austrian front collapsed along seventy miles. But this was only the beginning. As the rout of the central armies opened the flanks of the divisions immediately north and south of Brussilov's breakthrough, Conrad's troops folded all the way from Pinsk to the Romanian border, a distance of over 250 miles. It was then made clear beyond any shadow of doubt that the Slav troops of the Habsburg Empire would not fight against a victorious Slav army. All they wanted to do was surrender. Meanwhile, Conrad himself had been finally halted in the Asiago on 10 June, by reinforcements rushed by Cadorna along the superb railway system of Northern Italy, before the Brussilov offensive had had time to make its effect felt. It was now Conrad's turn to wildly appeal to Falkenhayn for help, which was of course embarrassing, as he himself had made Brussilov's offensive possible by diverting divisions from the Eastern front to Italy without telling Falkenhayn first, in revenge for Falkenhayn's not having consulted him before he had ordered the attack on Verdun. Conrad was not really having as good a war as he deserved. The Germans first suggested coldly that he move back to the Russian front the divisions he had unwisely transferred from thence to the Trentino; then they relented and let him have one German division from Macedonia, another from the Northern Russian front and, most important, two more divisions from France. The German relief was barely on its way when Cadorna opened a counter-offensive at Asiago on 16 June.

Conrad's battle plan had collapsed entirely. First he had helped to strangle the German effort at Verdun by refusing to move his heavy artillery from the Russian front to France; then he had produced the conditions for Brussilov's great breakthrough by transferring infantry divisions from Galicia to the Trentino; and now he had to prevent the loss of his gains at Asiago by rushing men back from Italy to Russia. Nor was this all. He had actually forced the Germans to weaken their own defences in the West, at a time when the British were about to attack on the Somme with an advantage of two to one in men and artillery, and with complete air superiority.

The Italian intervention had thus made all the difference. Cadorna's unrelenting sacrifice of Italy's armies had scarcely yet begun to draw the attentions of the Germans in his direction, for only ten battalions of German alpine troops had yet been moved to the Italian front.[21] What he had achieved was the total disruption of the Austrian contribution. Twenty-four Austrian divisions with over two thousand guns were tied up on the Italian front. Five German divisions had been sent from France and two from other sectors to plug the gaps produced in the Eastern front by Conrad's enterprise in the Asiago. There was no time when Germany could not have won the war with an extra twenty-nine divisions and no anxieties on the Italian frontier.

Cadorna unfortunately was hardly perceptive or flexible enough to take full advantage of an enemy's preoccupations. The Italian army admittedly needed a rest. Conrad's Asiago offensive had developed into the bloodiest encounter yet between the Kingdom of Italy and the Habsburg Empire. Casualties amounted in all to 147,000 Italians and 81,000 Austrians killed, wounded, missing and taken prisoner. Cadorna was none the less able to exploit his splendid rail services and his great fleet of Fiat cars to rush reserves back to Isonzo and mount a sixth assault before the Austrians expected him to be able to do so. Twenty-two Italian divisions took the field against only nine Austrian on 6 August. Their artillery preparation was still quite inadequate, however. Cadorna had enough light guns, but only heavies could make a useful impression on the Austrian defences, and of these Cadorna could assemble only one for every 440 yards of his front, whereas the British at the Somme had advanced under the protection of eight times that density of fire.

Allied pressure none the less kept the Germans and Austrians on the defensive on every fighting front for a few weeks at least. Brussilov sustained his heroic efforts in the East until about 20 September; the nightmare of attrition on the Somme ended finally on 18 November with casualties estimated at 650,000 German and 615,000 British and French; and Cadorna halted his sixth Battle of the Isonzo on 17 August after winning Italy's first noteworthy offensive victory since the preliminary campaigns of May–June 1915. He had lost another 100,000 men, but he had crossed the Isonzo at Gorizia. The front line on the Italian front had moved eastward a whole three miles.

This success convinced Cadorna that he was employing the correct methods. Not even Douglas Haig showed a more unrelenting dedication to the spirit of the offensive. He decided to spread Italy's war effort even more widely, sending 55,000 Italian troops to Salonika to join the 210,000 French, 180,000 British and 152,000 Serbs stationed there in addition to the 100,000-odd Italians already in Albania.[22] War was declared against Germany on 27 August, at the urgent demands of the Allies; and on 14 September Cadorna began the seventh Battle of the Isonzo. Meanwhile, Italian troops in Albania began to engage the Austrians pressing after the defeated Serbs. After twelve days of minimal progress, bad weather halted Cadorna's efforts briefly, but he resumed the assault between 10 and 12 October. Then a tenth battle was sustained in blizzard conditions from 1 to 14 November, while the Italian detachment in Albania advanced fifty miles from the Vijose river to link up with the other Allied forces advancing from Salonika to the Bulgarian border. The last three engagements succeeded in improving the Gorizia bridgehead only in the slightest degree. But they had helped to make a monumental contribution to Allied victory. Each new Italian effort precipitated a further desperate flood of Austrian reinforcements from the Eastern front. By the end of 1915 Cadorna's forty-eight divisions faced thirty-five Austrian divisions, or over half the total fighting strength of the Habsburg Empire.* And the Germans were coming too at last.

Cadorna was fully aware of the implications of the impending Russian disaster – the almost total collapse of the Romanians in the last quarter of 1916 had displayed sufficiently the German genius for converting defence into devastating attack. He therefore appealed urgently to British and French generals in an Allied conference in Rome in January 1917, that they should recognize Italy's needs which would consist of ten Anglo-French divisions and 400 more guns to secure Italy against a combined Austro-German offensive.[23] But the Western Allies had plans of their own. It had already been agreed at the third Chantilly Conference in December that the offensive plans of all Germany's enemies should be co-ordinated for a supreme effort in 1917. And as France's contribution was to be a great attack on the Aisne, to break the German armies in the field, General Nivelle, whose idea this had been, accordingly explained to Cadorna that not only would no French reinforcements be available, but the Italians would be required to deliver yet another offensive of their own, in order to prevent any transfer of Austro-German strength to the Western front.[24]

Cadorna could always be relied upon to carry out such a plan: he never had any other. But the Allied steamroller never looked like working according to plan. Although the Russians were first to sacrifice themselves, as ever, their offensive at Riga in January soon collapsed in the face of furious German resistance. The Western Allies hastened to conclude formally with Russia the agreement previously arrived at in May 1916, to divide Anatolia into spheres of interest among themselves, excluding Italy from any share in the spoils of the Turkish Empire. And with British forces in the Middle East already pressing victoriously on to Baghdad, before crumbling Turkish

* The Austrians at this time had a total of sixty-six divisions in the field on all fronts. An Austrian division amounted to fifteen battalions at full strength, compared with the twelve battalions of an Italian division, so the odds in fact were nearer to 48 to 44

resistance, they could feel confident in their power to bring this plan into effect. But backstage diplomacy of this kind could not suffice to keep the discredited Tsarist regime in power. Russia exploded in revolution on 12 March. Tsar Nicholas abdicated three days later.

These events did not, however, at first seem to herald the early departure of Russia from the war. It was even held possible that the Russians would fight better, now that they had some power to select leaders in whom they could have confidence. But there could be little doubt that the Western Allies had no time to waste. The British offensive, opened before Arras on 9 April, began as a fairly minor affair. Fourteen British divisions moved against seven German, backed by an artillery support more than twice as massive as had been accumulated for the Somme enterprise. But the fighting continued until 14 April; was resumed on 23 April; and did not terminate until 17 May, in which time the British casualty list had mounted to about 84,000 compared with 75,000 German.[25]

Meanwhile, the French had begun their 'act of brute force'. This plan involved far larger numbers than had been on the British front, but the margin of superiority was significantly less. Forty-six French divisions with 3,810 guns attempted to turn out forty-two German divisions with 2,451 guns, with notably more success than the British had had. The Germans admitted losses of 163,000, compared with French casualties of 110,701.[26] But the territorial gain of only four miles, was a great disappointment, and resulted in a loss of confidence among the soldiers which effectively paralyzed the French army for most of the remainder of the year. Then on 19 May the reconstituted Serb armies refused to participate in the planned Salonika offensive. Britain and Italy were effectively the only two Allied nations left capable of sustaining the war against the Central Powers.

Italy's new-found importance had already been recognized. Sonnino had been meeting British Prime Minister Lloyd George and French Foreign Minister Aristide Briand at St Jean de

Maurienne on 19 and 20 April when the disappointing news of Nivelle's offensive came in. Deciding that any price was worth paying at this stage for continued and active Italian participation, the British and French accordingly agreed to let the Italians have Smyrna, Adalia and all of Anatolia from the wreck of the Turkish Empire, without of course consulting the Russians either before or after – just as they agreed with the Russians a month earlier to divide Turkey up among themselves, without consulting the Italians.[27] They also consented to let Cadorna have at least a quarter of the guns he had asked for, the British supplying him with forty 6-inch howitzers at once, and a further twelve in July, along with one 9.2-inch weapon, and the French sending a dozen heavy batteries.[28] But French Foreign Minister Delcassé was not playing merely a double game, he was playing a triple one. Having given these undertakings to the Italians, he then assured Greek pro-Allied ex-Prime Minister Venizelos, who had established a rebel government in Crete,[29] that France did not want to see Italian power grow in the Mediterranean.[30] This was of course true, in that the only power that the French wished to see grow in the Mediterranean was their own. But Delcassé's primary concern was to encourage Venizelos to engineer the removal of pro-German King Constantine from Greece, where the Allies were bogged down again in the Salonika 'bird-cage'. There were no limits to the enterprise of French duplicity.

Cadorna of course guessed nothing of this. Nobody ever had less talent or desire to read the mind of another human being. On 12 May, having amassed again a near two-to-one superiority in man power, and a concentration and weight of artillery comparable with what was deemed necessary to support attacks on the other fronts, he hurled his forces into their tenth assault on the Isonzo. Thirty-two Italian divisions with 2,638 guns assailed seventeen Austrian divisions, with 1,402 guns. The collision reached new heights of slaughter, with the Italians suffering total losses of about the same order as those endured by the British over a similar period at Arras, and far in excess of

Nivelle's. The tenth Battle of the Isonzo cost Italy 36,000 dead, 96,000 wounded and 25,000 prisoners. The actual Italian loss of life was higher than that of the British and French put together, thanks to the great strength of the Austrian defences, the lack of heavy artillery with which to subdue them, and the fact that shells landing on the rocky surfaces of the battlefield exploded on contact instead of burying themselves as they did in the less resistant soil of France, where they lost most of their destructive effect.

But it was not only the Italians who were suffering. The Austrians had looked forward gaily and confidently to continuing their unbroken procession of victory in the open field, forgetting how only La Mamora's generalship had saved them from defeat at Custozza. The very last thing that they could have anticipated from the Italians was an unrelenting sequence of bloody offensive battles of attrition, sustained over two years, at a cost to their own armies of over half a million dead so far. Austrian defences were repeatedly on the point of collapse after Cadorna's onslaughts, and were saved from disaster only by the Italians' lack of sufficient heavy artillery to blast a clear hole in the fortifications opposed to them. Conrad duly rushed a further three divisions to his threatened Southern front, and the Austrian counter-attack on 28 May recovered most of the insignificant gains won by Cadorna's tenth assault. But the trial of strength was not over yet. Cadorna, who had also begun concentrating still more men and guns, was likewise compelled to disperse his forces. Then on 12 June Western intrigues with Venizelos forced King Constantine of Greece to abdicate. The implications were obvious: Athens, a new challenger to Italy's Balkan ambitions, would bring its insatiable territorial appetite to the victory banquet. Italy was in a position to lose exactly the rewards for which it had entered the war.

Rome took precautionary measures immediately. When General Giacinto Ferrero proclaimed in Valona the independence of Albania as a free and sovereign state, under Italian protection, events moved quickly. On 1 July Brussilov, now commander-in-chief under Kerensky of all the Russian armies, launched his last forlorn offensive in Galicia, the only offensive of the war in which Russian troops advanced under cover of an artillery barrage heavier than their enemies could deploy against them; Greece entered the war on the following day; and Italian forces in Albania were augmented to a total of five divisions.[31] Italy's allies had now become more troublesome than its enemies. But the problems of the Balkans were only beginning: on 20 July Serb Premier Pasić and Ante Trumbić, former Mayor of Spalato and subsequently President of the Jugoslav Committee, signed the Declaration of Corfu, creating a new state of Yugoslavia, to comprise Serbia, Montenegro and the Southern Slav provinces of the Habsburg Empire. A vast, new independent power was about to be born across the Adriatic. The prospect of Allied victory was beginning to look almost as bad for Italy as the prospect of defeat.

But victory had still to be won. The Kerensky offensive finally broke down on 24 July. On 31 July the British made their bid in the third Battle of Ypres, hurling against nine German divisions twelve divisions supported by 2,266 cannon, with one heavy gun to every twenty yards of their front – the most awesome concentration of fire power yet. Then on 19 August was opened the greatest Allied offensive of the year so far, when Cadorna delivered his eleventh, biggest, most successful and last assault on the Isonzo front, with fifty-two divisions and 5,000 guns massed along the twenty-five miles from Tolmino to the Adriatic. This time it almost worked. For one thing, he had the guns. Italian industry had equipped him with 1,600 heavies, which, with the extra 100 provided by the British and French, gave him one heavy piece for every twenty-six yards of front. The air service's contribution, which was huge and sustained, was also invaluable: on the opening day of the offensive eighty-five Capronis staged the biggest bombing attack of the war, and during the next ten days 1,474 sorties in all were flown over the Austrian lines, at a cost of eighty-one pilots killed. These efforts brought Cadorna greater successes than he had achieved in all the ten previous assaults put together. General Luigi Capello's second army smashed into the Austrian defences to a depth of six miles on the Bainsizza Plateau, driving the Austrians, fighting better than they had ever fought on any front, out of their prepared positions and into open, broken country. Then, seeing that Conrad's troops were on the point of collapse, Cadorna gave the order for the pursuit. But as infantry cannot advance without guns, and the artillery had been left far in the rear, Cadorna was forced to halt the advance to allow the heavies to be brought up. What he had not realized was that the roads were hopeless, and with the inability of the troops to manage their traffic, chaos was soon produced, and the impetus of the offensive was lost for good. Cadorna had almost broken Conrad's armies: he had quite broken his own. Italian casualties had soared in the four weeks' bloody fighting to a new peak of 166,000, including 40,000 dead. And the impact of this fearful blood-letting was enormously exacerbated by Cadorna's fatally shortsighted policy of culling the best troops from all battalions into special brigades of shock troops, the *Arditi,* who were used to spearhead each successive assault. This method, although unsuccessful in breaching the Austrian defences, had been all too successful in killing off the best fighting men of Italy.

Even in spite of this Cadorna might still have been able to rally his men for the one last blow that would have set Italy free from the Alps to the Adriatic, had he been given the chance to deliver it. But the mammoth Italian sacrifice had at last achieved a diversion of German as well as Austrian man power: the new Emperor, Charles I, fully aware that his armies in Italy were in extremity, appealed urgently to the Germans to provide replacements for those Austrian divisions still serving in Russia, so that the whole strength of the Habsburg Empire could be brought to bear on Italy. He also hoped that it might be easier to contrive a separate peace with the Allies if he could manage to group all his armies on one front, under Austrian commanders. The Germans, however, appreciated this too, and naturally were not inclined to co-operate. Neither were they particularly concerned, having no grounds to believe that the Austrians could manage by themselves to knock Italy out of the war, even if they were allowed to devote all their remaining powers to the task. Only German technology could provide the fire power needed to blast a gap in strong trench positions garrisoned by a numerically stronger army; only German determination and enterprise could keep an offensive pouring on through every available avenue for advance; only German organization and ruthlessness could keep the guns rolling up in support of the ever-advancing infantry. Ludendorff accordingly despatched General Otto von Below to the Italian front, with seven specially trained divisions, to form a new fourteenth army, with nine crack Austrian divisions, skilled in both mountain warfare and offensive tactics of infiltration.

Once again Cadorna had ample warning of what was in store. His first move was to order Capello to prepare to meet an Austro-German counter-offensive. But Cadorna's subordinates had long since decided to ignore the requests of their disagreeable commander, and Capello, who was almost as obstinate as Cadorna, was sick of taking the offensive himself before the enemy could move. He had in any event adequate reason for doubting that even the Germans would attempt to attack in conditions of driving snow and rain.

But this was exactly what von Below proposed to do. Not only would the foul weather help to blind the Italian defences, it would at the same time lull the anxieties of the Italian commanders. And to compensate for his inferiority in numbers of sixteen divisions against Capello's twenty-five he needed all the elements of surprise that he could achieve. Everything worked according to plan. A short and intense bombardment of high-explosive and gas shells was delivered on the morning of 24 October against the Italian positions unprepared, disorganized, drenched in rain, and blanketed with sleet and cloud. As with the Austrians facing Brussilov, it was hours before the high command fully appreciated that an offensive was taking place. By that time, Capello's front-line troops were already in full flight from an enemy who had swept invisibly all round them. Von Below's attackers had covered twelve miles by the end of the day. It was the second most rapid day's advance of the war.

There was every reason for the Italian collapse. They were the first to experience a new style of attack which the Germans were to use in France with even more success in the following year;[32] they were utterly unprepared, thanks to the weather, to the perfected German planning, and to the total lack of harmony among their commanders; and they were demoralized and physically depleted by the eleven fearful battles they had been subjected to on this front by a callous and inflexible leader. But the main cause of the rout was simply a total war-weariness among Cadorna's men. They had sacrificed themselves continuously for two and a half years, in the interests of totally indifferent allies; they had seen their few gains won at such a cost wiped out in a few hours; and they had had enough. Nobody had ever accused the Italians of being unintelligent; and intelligent men were not likely to go on fighting in those conditions, without being given some extraordinarily good reason for doing so. The second army had given up the war.

This was the kind of situation at which Cadorna was at his best, once his rigid mind managed to appreciate what was happening. This took two days. At first he tried to check the Austro-German flood with counter-attacks, but these were rendered ineffective by lack of reserves, the weather and the fact that roads leading to the battlefield were blocked by the 400,000 deserters of the second army. Then on 27 October he ordered a retreat to the Tagliamento, where he hoped to form a defensive line with the unbroken third and fourth armies. But the Tagliamento was in flood, the Germans were outflanking it already, and the speed of the rout had become such that the second army had crossed the river and was heading towards the Piave, twenty to forty miles further south, before the third army had managed to cross the Isonzo.

This calamity of Caporetto, so called after the village on the Isonzo where von Below's troops effected their first crossing, had at least one beneficial result: the Western Allies awoke abruptly to the need for reinforcements on the Italian front. And the situation could hardly have been more serious. The armies of the Allies were one by one collapsing under the strain. The Russians were in revolt; the French were in a state of mutiny; the Serbs were refusing to fight; and the Italians had deserted. It was decided on 28 October to send six French and five British divisions to Italy at once, even though it was quite likely they would be too late. Only the Italians would be in time to hold the line of the Piave twenty-five miles behind the Tagliamento and only fifteen in front of Venice.

Neither their enemies nor their allies expected them to be able to do so. The second army had virtually ceased to exist – 10,000 men had been killed, 30,000 wounded and 293,000 taken prisoner, as well as the 400,000 who had abandoned their rifles and the war and were heading home, having made their individual separate peace. Cadorna made matters still worse, if that were possible, by a typically offensive Order of the Day, claiming that the second army 'cravenly withdrew without fighting or ignominiously surrendered to the enemy . . .'[33] This did not improve the military situation, but it at least brought down the government. Salandra, tired, aloof and ill-at-ease coping with a war which he had not been prepared to face in 1914, yielded office to Vittorio Emanuele Orlando, less dignified, less personally impressive, but more supple and adept in managing a parliamentary assembly. And meanwhile the Duke of Aosta's third army was winning its race with von Below. The Austro-German pursuit was delayed by flooded marshlands and pouring rain, by the heroism of the Italian marines who covered Aosta's retreat, and by their own exhaustion after a week's marching and fighting. Armoured cars or cavalry could have cut off and destroyed the third army, but these were exactly what the Austro-Germans lacked. What they got instead was relentless covering actions by the Italians' own cavalry, under the wild hunt of the Capronis and Savoias through the rainswept skies.

Below none the less managed to outflank the line of the Tagliamento in the North, almost as soon as Aosta had crossed it. But Cadorna had a precious two days in which to reform part at least of his broken army. It was just long enough. Aosta's men would still fight. So would the air service, the remains of the *Arditi*, and the crack Bersaglieri regiments, who were assigned the task of compelling the deserters of the second army to rejoin Italy's war. Capello's ex-soldiers, innocently believing that they would be allowed to leave a war by simply walking away from it, were met on the other side of the Tagliamento by black-plumed Bersaglieri who either shot them out of hand or drafted them in orderly fashion to the rear, to be regrouped into fighting units. It did not take Capello's men long to get the message. They could expect to have some chance against the Austrians; they had none against the firing squads of the Bersaglieri. The desertion was over. On 3 and 4 November the Italian army turned to fight for the first time since 24 October, and at San Vito they succeeded in repulsing von Below's attempt to cross the river. It was an army capable of resistance that Cadorna led back from the Tagliamento on 7 November.

But the question was still to find a line on which a shattered force could hope to resist what was now a vastly stronger enemy. Cadorna made a brief rally on the shallow line of the Livenza on 7 and 8 November, then fell back to the Piave, but this was 'not a front which a general would select had he any choice'.[34] The river was a 'strong line only towards its mouth, a weak and difficult line in the centre, and no line at all in its upper glens'.[35] But it was at least anchored on one flank by the Adriatic and on the other by the mountain fortress of Monte Grappa; Cadorna had had the foresight in months past to prepare gun emplacements and dug-outs to provide a forward defence for Venice; and the symbolic significance of the stream was enormous. D'Annunzio displayed once again his effortless command of inspiring bombast. 'Are there', he asked, 'in Italy other living waters – I will not think of them. . . . Forget all else for the moment and remember only that this water is for us the water of life, regenerative like that of baptism. . . . It runs beside the walls, and past the doors, and through the streets of all the cities of Italy; it runs past the threshold of all our dwellings; it safeguards from the destroyer all our altars and all our hearts.'[36] But the most eloquent words delivered on the occasion were Cadorna's own, conveyed to the men of the first, third and fourth armies on 9 November, the day of his own dismissal from the post of Chief of General Staff in favour of General Armando Diaz: 'We have taken the inflexible decision to defend here the honour and life of Italy. Every soldier must know what is the cry and command issuing from the conscience of the whole Italian people: to die and not to yield.'[37]

Diaz himself was ready enough to do just that. But his prospects of doing so with victory were unpromising in the extreme. For the first time in the war, the Italians were outnumbered along the whole of their front; 423 of their battalions stood on the Piave with 3,500 guns, to face the attack of 652 Austrian and eighty-four German battalions with 7,000 guns. The assault began on the Monte Grappa position on 11 November. On the following day von Below's fourteenth army crossed the Piave eighteen miles from the sea. Four more attempts to cross were repelled on 14 November, but in the meantime the Austrians had made further gains in the mountains on the left flank of the Italian line. Another assault on the right flank gained the Austro-Germans a second bridge-head across the Piave, after which continuous see-saw fighting went on for twenty days, with the Italians, apparently, gradually being worn down.

But in fact every day increased Diaz's chances. Guns were pouring out of Italy's factories to replace the 3,200 that had been lost in the retreat; another 130 battalions had been created out of Capello's deserters, augmented by almost untrained seventeen- and eighteen-year-olds from the base camps; and the British and French were on the way. A tremendous Austrian offensive was launched in the Monte Grappa region on 6 December, under a barrage from 2,000 guns firing on twelve miles of front, but it achieved only partial success. Other attacks maintained over the next twelve days put the Austrians in a position to outflank the Italian mountain defences, but then Italian counter-attacks on 22 December recovered the southern slopes and substantially restored the situation. Meanwhile, the Germans had withdrawn four of their seven divisions to the Western front, winter weather in the mountains making further action there impossible in any event; the bridge-heads across the Piave could not be expanded in the face of dedicated resistance by Italian marines, supported by ceaseless shelling from monitors and floating batteries anchored offshore;* and the French and British divisions, which on 12 December had been formed into a general reserve began to move into the line. The First World War had been won and lost on the Piave. There would be no Austrian army for the spring offensive in France in 1918.

The Anglo-French intervention in Italy was distinctly restrained at first. The British had begun to prepare defensive positions behind the line of the Piave on 4 December, and on 30 December French infantry and British artillery co-operated in a small patrol action near the mountains. Their main contribution was to enable the Italians to move divisions from quiet areas of the front, where they were replaced by the British and French, in order to strengthen their lines still in danger in the mountains. The most significant impact on the actual fighting was made by seventy-two fighters of the Royal Flying Corps, who shot down sixty-four of the 213 Austrian and German aircraft destroyed on the Italian front that year, for a loss of only twelve of their own number.[38]

Meanwhile the war at sea had suddenly swung spectacularly in favour of the Italians. As the Austrians had shown no disposition since the beginning of 1916 to risk meeting the superior Italian fleet in a surface action, Admiral di Revel's problem all along had been to find some means of striking at a hostile fleet

* The Italians had four monitors armed with 15 in. guns, four with 12 in. guns, and over ninety floating batteries, armed with a variety of lighter weapons (Fraccaroli, pp. 213–227)

which persisted in remaining in its own heavily protected harbours. An unsuccessful attempt to assail the Austrians from the air was made on 23 September 1917 when Lieutenant Ridolfi, flying a Caproni Ca47, launched torpedoes from the air at Austrian ships in Pola harbour. The missiles struck home, but their charges failed to explode. But there was now available in large numbers a more reliable weapon, the little MAS-boats – about twelve tons each, with a speed of from 22 to 25 knots and carrying two 17.7-inch torpedoes – which had begun to haunt the Adriatic from the beginning of 1916. MAS 6 broke into the roadstead of Durazzo by night on four occasions. Two other MAS-boats skirmished indecisively on 16 November with Austrian ships hovering in the Gulf of Venice. Then on 10 December the Bersaglieri of the sea gained their first portentous triumph. MAS 9 and 13 entered the harbour of Trieste by night; cut through eight cables strung for defence across the entry to the roadstead; and torpedoed two Austrian battleships, actually sinking the twenty-four-year-old pre-dreadnought *Vienna*, of 5,600 tons displacement and armed with four 9.4-inch guns.

The *Vienna* had probably never constituted a very serious threat to any of the world's navies, even when it was afloat. Nevertheless, the sheer daring of the Italian seamen, displayed at a time when Italy needed all the courage it could muster, amply justified the acclamations which their exploit received – and they were not restrained. D'Annunzio proclaimed that the Italian navy had shown that it was ever ready to dare the undareable. Di Revel affirmed that Italy had 'the honour of having developed the MAS as an instrument of war', and had 'achieved the triumph of the smallest maritime weapon over the greatest, of David over Goliath'.[39]

Even greater things were in store for the MAS. But in the meantime the political and military situation of the First World War had again changed completely. Fighting was ended on the Russian front on 2 December 1917, and the Central Powers were accordingly able to regroup their forces. At the beginning of 1916, fifty-nine German and forty-four Austrian divisions, 103 in all, were opposed to 126 Russian divisions in the East; 100 German divisions were opposed to fifty-six British, 101 French and the equivalent of six Belgian divisions, or 163 in all, in the West; and twenty-two Austrian divisions were opposed to Cadorna's thirty-nine in Italy. This picture had changed significantly by the first quarter of 1918. The war entered its last phase with 182 German and two Austrian divisions against ninety-nine French, fifty-eight British, nine American, five Belgian and two Portuguese, or 173 in all, in the West; and fifty-eight Austrian divisions against fifty-two Italian, three British and two French in Italy.

It was a sufficiently serious matter that the Western Allies would now for the first time have to meet the Germans, who were admittedly almost exhausted by now, on something like equal terms. There was no question of leaving the Anglo-French divisions in Italy to meet the Austrian spring offensive on the Piave. It was rather for Diaz to consider how much of his own fully-extended strength he could dare to despatch to strengthen the line in France, where 2,203 Italian volunteers had already been serving since 1914 in the 'Rossa Avanguardia delle Argonne', under the condottiere Beppino Garibaldi. Orlando had already agreed on 11 November 1917 to the principle of transferring Italian divisions to France when the need arose, in return for the Western Allies agreeing to send help to Italy during the crisis on the Piave. In the meantime 60,000 Italian soldiers under General Guiseppe Tarditi, and three squadrons of Capronis were sent to France, while the French withdrew four of their six divisions from the Italian front, and the British called back two of the five that they had sent in November 1917.[40]

They got back just in time. On 21 March the Germans began the first of their last desperate bids for victory, assailing the British on the Somme with seventy-one divisions against twenty-nine, and 2,508 heavy guns against 976.[41] Ludendorff's men advanced forty miles in eight days. It was then that the diplomatic cohesion between the Western Allies and Italy was suddenly called in question. Members of the independence movements among the Southern Slav peoples of the Habsburg Empire met secretly with Serb authorities in Cattaro in March, to agree on the formation of a new Yugoslav state after victory. Then on 8 and 10 April 1918 a Congress of representatives of the Subject Nationalities of Austria-Hungary meeting in Campodoglio approved, with the Italian parlimentarian Torre, the Pact of Rome, under which

> '. . . the representatives of the Italian people and of the Jugoslav people in particular agree (*inter alia*) as follows:
>
> 1. In the relations between the Italian nation and the nation of the Serbs, Croats and Slovenes – known also under the name of the Jugoslav nation – the representatives of the two peoples recognise that the unity and independence of the Jugoslav nation is a vital interest to Italy, just as the completion of Italian national unity is a vital interest of the Jugoslav nation. . . .
>
> 2. They declare that the liberation of the Adriatic Sea and its defence against every present and future enemy is a vital interest of the two peoples. . . .
>
> 4. To such racial groups of one people as it may be found necessary to include within the frontiers of the other there shall be recognised the right to their language, culture, and moral and economic interests.'[42]

The Pact of Rome had of course no official status as far as the Italians were concerned. Although Torre had the backing of a number of Italian deputies and senators, he could not speak for the government as a whole. And in fact any responsible Italian government could only be appalled at the prospect of seeing founded across the Adriatic a huge Yugoslav state, consisting precisely of those national groups who were fighting most enthusiastically against Italy in the ranks of the Austrian army, and dominated by the Serbs, the most recalcitrant and resolute fighters in Europe. It appeared that Franz Ferdinand's ambitions were after all being realized. The authority of Vienna beyond the Dalmatian coast would be replaced by that of Belgrade. Italy would have sacrificed more blood and treasure than any of the other Allies, and have gained in return almost nothing that it fought for. Italy's whole aim in entering the war was to replace Austrian domination in the Balkans. This aim had been resented by the British, intrigued against and betrayed by the French, and challenged head-on by the Russians. And now the Slav peoples themselves were against the idea. One could hardly deny that they had a perfect right to be so, but no more could one assert that a Great Power fights for nothing.

Meanwhile there was still a war to be won. On 9 April thirty-two German divisions struck south of Armentieres against eleven British, inflicting over 300,000 casualties on the British and thereby achieving almost as great a victory as at Carporetto. Diaz promptly rushed two big divisions to the Western front, so that on 27 May, by the time the third great German offensive was delivered across the Aisne 131,000 Italians were there to strengthen the French line.

This encounter was to be Ludendorff's greatest success in the West. His infantry advanced about fifty miles, until they were halted on the Marne at Chateau-Thierry by massive and enthusiastic American divisions. Both sides had meanwhile urgently been pressing their allies in Italy and the Balkans to take some action. The Austrians had by now managed to assemble sixty divisions with 7,500 guns, a third as many men and nearly half as many guns as Ludendorff could deploy against all his enemies in the West,[43] whereas Diaz's forces had been reduced by transfers to France to fifty-six divisions with 7,000 guns.[44] It was not enough with which to take the offensive, but it would be more than enough to repel one. And in the meantime the Italian navy had spectacularly smashed the Central Powers' plan for a joint naval offensive in the Mediterranean with the most brilliant torpedo-boat operations of the war. On 14 May Commander Pellegrini piloted MAS *Grillo* into Pola harbour, under cover of a raid by Italian naval sea-planes, and torpedoed the Austrian dreadnaught *Viribus Unitis,* the flagship of the Habsburg fleet, displacing 20,010 tons and armed with twelve twelve-inch guns. The *Viribus Unitis* was not sunk, but only badly holed, and Pellegrini and his crew were taken prisoner. But they had prevented the ship from taking part in the last great sortie of the Austrian navy on 9 June, when its sisters *Svent Istvan* and *Tegetthoff* sailed into the Adriatic with an escort of ten destroyers, in the hope of linking up in the eastern Mediterranean with units of the Russian navy, captured by the Germans and about to be sailed by them through the Dardanelles to challenge Allied naval power in the Aegean and the Adriatic. Both seas were now swarming with about 270 MAS-boats. Two met up with the Austrian battle-ships and their escorts on the night of 10 June, and proceeded to sail along in their company with supreme effrontery, manoeuvring at leisure into the best attacking positions until at last recognized by the Austrians. They then turned savagely, torpedoed the two battleships, blew the nose off an interfering destroyer, and disappeared into the darkness unharmed, leaving the last two capital ships of the Austrian navy sinking behind them. Lissa had been avenged.

This was undoubtedly the cheapest naval victory of the war. It certainly did nothing to improve the morale of the Austrian high command, still squabbling irreconcilably over who was to have the honour of dealing the last fatal blow to the national enemy. German casualties in France soared to over 600,000, while the Archduke Eugene tried to mediate between Conrad, now demoted to subordinate rank, who insisted on being allowed to deliver the *coup de grâce* in the Trentino, and the rather more successful Slav general Boroevic, who argued in favour of victory on the Piave. Eugene finally reached a decision, as the fourth German offensive in the Noyon-Montidier region ground bloodily to a halt in the face of brilliantly effective French resistance. His solution was to divide reserves equally between his two snarling generals. Vienna could always be relied upon to screw things up.

Attacked all along the line, the Italian front held all along the line. Conrad made marginal gains in the West on the first day, and Boroevic succeeded in crossing the Piave at three points, to a depth of three miles. But this was as far as either of them got. The two armies flew at each other's throats for eight more days. Once again the Italians triumphed in the very kind of blood-soaked slugging match which they might have been expected to be least fitted temperamentally to endure. The Austrians succumbed, as they had before, to the effectiveness of massed Italian artillery, the mounting fury of Italian air attacks and the exigencies of the Piave itself, which rose sharply to threaten their floating bridges.[45] Boroevic sadly called the attack off over 22–23 June. The beaten armies of the Habsburg Empire were back on the other side of the river on the following day.

Austria had lost the war finally for Germany and for itself. Italy had guaranteed its own survival and that of the Entente. Even thirty Austrian divisions could have given Ludendorff victory in the West. At the very least they could have checked the Allied outflanking movement through the Balkans and enabled the Germans to stand on the defensive in France forever. But the failure on the Piave now meant that the Emperor Charles would need every available man and gun to contain the Italians. The war was over. All that remained was to stop the fighting.

It was indeed the peace that was being fought for now. Italy's victory on the Piave had made it that much less necessary for the Entente to think seriously of honouring the provisions of the Treaty of London. And now a vast and alien presence was beginning to impose its own will upon a weakened Europe.

Although the United States had entered the war primarily in response to the devastating threat to the American economy presented by the unrestricted submarine campaign launched by the Germans, one other problem had vexed President Wilson and his advisers ever since the outbreak of hostilities in 1914. This was that a posture of neutrality, which was the only one politically viable at the time, might well jeopardize the future of the United States as a Great Power. A neutral America would be in no position to influence the terms of the eventual peace settlement in Europe. It would indeed have to live with the fact that the victor of the European contest would emerge as unchallengeably the greatest and most influential power on earth. America's own hopes of world power would effectively be strangled at birth.

And ironically these hopes might have been more difficult to fulfil if the Americans had in fact entered the war on the winning side, as they had believed they were doing, for in this case any material assistance they could render the Entente would be both small and superfluous. But they entered to find the Russians opting for a separate peace; the British facing starvation as a result of the submarine blockade; the French army virtually on strike; and the Italians racing against annihilation from Carporetto to the Piave. In these circumstances it could well seem as if almost any assistance from the United States might be absolutely essential to the cause of the Entente, which in turn would entitle Washington to impose its own concepts of a peace settlement upon both its co-belligerents and its enemies.

Although American help had been notably insubstantial so far, its effect on morale was unquestionable. The Entente Powers could continue the fight in the knowledge that virtually inexhaustible supplies of man power and material would be coming to their assistance from across the Atlantic. Time was therefore undeniably on their side. But it was not until after the United States had been in the war for a whole year that the first American division saw action in France; and barely 300,000 American troops in all had crossed the Atlantic by the end of April 1918.

Nevertheless, the United States had already begun to impose its own will upon the shape of post-war Europe. The Wilson administration had been prepared to consider an accommodation with the Habsburg Empire for as long as it appeared possible that the Empire itself might survive as a viable factor in European affairs. By the second quarter of 1918, however, American sympathies had become firmly committed to the Slav Revolutionary Movement. On the very day that the last of Boroevic's beaten troops recrossed the Piave, Wilson's Secretary of State Robert Lansing declared that 'the position of the United States Government is that all branches of the Slav race should be completely freed from German and Austrian rule'.[46] The British and French duly fell into line. British Foreign Secretary Balfour in a letter to President Wilson had already referred to the Treaty of London as 'regrettable'.[47] He then proclaimed on 25 July British association with the goal of 'the independence and unity of all Serbs, Croats and Slovenes in a single state'.[48] This was even worse from the Italian viewpoint than Lansing's intervention, as the Treaty of London had envisaged three-quarters of a million Serbs and Croats falling under Italian rule in Dalmatia. Meanwhile, Foch continued to press for an Italian offensive to follow up the victory on the Piave.

But Diaz, doughty, prosaic and humane, was unconvinced that he could attempt successfully from the South, with fewer men and guns, the crossing that Conrad and Boroevic had failed to accomplish with their stronger armies from the North.

Diaz accordingly waited stolidly and regrouped his forces, while guns and aircraft poured from Italy's factories to give him at last a decisive technical superiority over the Austrians. Then, when the last German drive in the West was halted around Rheims by twenty-three French, nine American, two British and two Italian divisions,[49] 910 Italians sailed for Tien-Tsin on 27 July, along with 4,500 British and 1,000 French troops to establish a Western presence in Asia;[50] and on 9 August Vienna became the first capital of the Central Powers to be attacked from the air.

The attack was indeed purely a symbolic affair. D'Annunzio assembled a flight of nine fast new Savoias; rallied the spirits of his crews with the formidable call: 'Let us challenge the future and the unknown, O Comrades, with our battle cry: Eia, eia, eia, Alala'; and led them on a 625-mile round trip to Vienna. One aircraft was brought down through engine failure. The other returned safely, having dropped on the gloom-ridden Habsburg capital not bombs, but bundles of the most remarkable pamphlet ever delivered by any means, written of course by D'Annunzio:

'Sul vente di vittoria che si leva dai fiume
della liberta, non siamo venuti se non per la
giaoia dell'ardezza, non siamo venuti se non per
la prova di quel che potremo osare e fare quando
vorremo, nell'ora che sieglieremo. Il rombo della
giovane ala non somiglia a quello del bronze funebre,
nel cielo mattutino. Tuttavia la bela audacia
sospende fra Santi Stefano e il Graben una sentenza
*non revocabili, O Viennesi.**

It was all perfectly true. Individual Austrian airmen were certainly a match for any of their Italian opponents. But Italian aviation backed up by the R.F.C. contingent had long since secured almost total command of the skies over the battlefield. The commander of the Austrian second army admitted bitterly that: 'The superiority of the Italian aviation is unquestionable in numbers as in quality. . . . Their courage, enterprise and resolve, with rare offensive spirit, provoked panic and demoralization among our troops.'[51] Even more demoralizing must have been the comparative ineffectiveness of the Austrian air force. When in 1918 the Italians made 1,382 raids over the Austrian lines, shooting down 647 Austrian aircraft for a loss of only thirty-two of their own, the Austrians were able to retaliate with only 145 raids.[52] Douhet eagerly proposed that the air offensive against the Central Powers be developed to include

* Youth is a matter of viewpoint. Italy's military wings were really older than anybody's. D'Annunzio was fifty-five at the time of the raid

massive attacks against their centres of production. Caproni offered to put his Ca33 at the disposal of all the Allied air forces for the purpose of such a campaign. It was undoubtedly the best and most versatile bombing aircraft in the world, but it was a little scarce for the job. Caproni's factories had increased their rate of production from twenty-eight airframes in 1915 to 320 in 1918. However, Douhet calculated that some 5,000 Ca33s would be required for a really destructive air offensive, and the war was not likely to last long enough for Italy to build so many.[53]

For Emperor Charles was now looking for a way to get out of the war quickly, before the Italians were able to make their bid for victory. As the German armies began their unchecked retreat in France, he approached the Allies for an exchange of views on the subject of a separate peace. This was rejected by the Americans, who had now virtually committed themselves to contriving the dissolution of the Habsburg Empire, which Charles was not wholly ready to contemplate. It was obviously time for Italy to safeguard its own position. Sonnino reasserted Italy's adherence to the Treaty of London, while Thaon di Revel stepped up the naval offensive in the Adriatic, bombarding Durazzo on 26 September and 2 October. But it was not only Italy which was concerned with what was left of the Austrian navy. The Slav crews of the Habsburg ships in Pola, who were effectively in a state of mutiny and prepared to seize these ships for the future Yugoslav navy, sent emissaries to Italy who announced their readiness to seize the ships and bring them over to the Entente, on condition that they remained in Yugoslav control after victory. Sonnino promptly arrested the emissaries and held them imprisoned until after the Armistice. He also refused to free some 18,000 Austrian prisoners of war of Slav nationality, who expressed a desire to fight for the Allied cause.[54] Meanwhile, Charles again approached the Allies, seeking Wilson's approval to an armistice based on the American President's own 'Fourteen Points', and promising autonomy to the Slav peoples of the Empire. Sonnino hastened to affirm that Italy did not consider that the Fourteen Points had even applied to Austria-Hungary anyway. But Italy was saved embarrassment by the Americans' own commitment to the cause of Slav nationalism. Wilson replied that the mere granting of autonomy would not by itself provide an acceptable basis for peace talks. The Slav National Committees then took the play away from Vienna on the following day by asserting the supremacy of the Serb, Croat and Slovene peoples over all the southern Slav portions of the Habsburg Empire.[55] It was the signal for internal revolt.[56] But before the revolutionaries could effectively seize power Diaz had at last begun to move. It was the anniversary of Caparetto.

Diaz's margin of strength was greater than that of Conrad and Boroevic when they had made their unsuccessful bid for victory in June. He had assembled fifty-six Italian divisions, three British and two French, as well as some Czech and American units, or roughly sixty-one in all, with a front-line air striking force of 553 Italian, eighty British and twenty French aircraft, and a massive park of 7,700 guns. Opposed to him were fifty-seven Austrian divisions, with 564 aircraft and 6,300 guns.[57] His plan was to use the Italian fourth army to draw the Austrian reserves away by an opening feint attack in the western mountains. The main effort would, however, be made along the line of the Piave itself by the eighth army of fourteen Italian divisions, flanked by the tenth army of two British and two Italian divisions, and the twelfth army of three Italian and one French.

Neither was fighting for a military victory, in the strict sense of the word. The First World War had already been decided, in the two battles of the Piave. The Italians were fighting to ensure themselves a dominant position in south-eastern Europe before the Yugoslavs, the Greeks and the Americans could beat them to it; the Austrians had nothing to fight for except honour. It was enough to stave off defeat for three more days. The only gains made on the first two days were those of the British and Italian detachments of the tenth army, which succeeded in establishing themselves on islands in the Piave – the fourth army had lost 25,000 without breaching the Austrian positions in the mountains. But on 27 October the British divisions of the tenth army and the French of the twelfth, under cover of a whirlwind attack by 342 Italian aircraft, managed to secure small bridgeheads across the river. Charles desperately announced his readiness for peace on almost any terms. But on 28 October, as Czechoslovakia declared its independence of the dissolving Habsburg Empire, the Italian eighth army, supported by 266 aircraft, drove across the Piave between the British and French bridgeheads.

The race was on. The southern Slav provinces were already rapidly amalgamating with Serbia into a huge new Yugoslav state. Serb armies, released by the collapse of Bulgaria, were marching towards their old capital, Belgrade. The Croatian Diet had assumed control of Fiume, to which they were indeed entitled under the terms of the Treaty of London. And now the Emperor Charles, in a last bid for Slav friendship, as well as a last attempt to deny the Italians the fruits of victory, presented the Habsburg fleet to the Yugoslavs, at the same time sending emissaries directly to Diaz to arrange an armistice.

Orlando and Sonnino were equal to the challenge. The Austrian emissaries were stalled off with the excuse that their credentials were not in order, while Diaz loosed his cavalry and armoured cars in a wild attack on Trieste and the Alps, and the MAS-boats put to sea again. In a formidable *coup,* Palucci and Rossetti managed to sink at last not only *Viribus Unitis,* but also the Yugoslav admiral and crew who had just come aboard to take advantage of Charles' offer.[58] Diaz finally agreed to an armistice with the routed Austrians at Villa Giusta on 3 November, insisting on their acceptance of the frontiers conceded to Italy under the terms of the Treaty of London, without the slightest reference to the interests of the Slavs.[59] On the same day, di Revel's ships landed Bersaglieri in Trieste and Pola, seized the Austrian ships still in harbour in those ports, and sailed them back to Italy, where di Revel grandiloquently hailed 'The arrival of this navy which yields without fighting . . . [which] could avoid action, but not defeat and surrender. . . . The Navy of Italy,' he continued, 'had revived and reaffirmed the glorious tradition of the Navy of St Mark.'[60] It had won a campaign as brutally one-sided as the one it was to lose twenty-five years later: at a cost of only seven submarines and twelve M.A.S., the Italians had sunk three Austrian battleships, three destroyers, eleven submarines and fourteen auxiliaries. And now di Revel's victorious ships were at work to seize the former possessions of Venice for the Kingdom of Italy. An Italian naval squadron seized Zara on 7 November, while Italian troops swept north from Scutari in the south and east into Slovenia and Carinthia in the north, ignoring the territorial limts agreed upon at Villa Giusta.[61] As Diaz's men began to move towards the Slovenian capital of Ljubljana, the Yugoslavs took the only course open to them. General mobilization was declared on 9 November. Shortly afterwards a warning was issued by Trumbic's military expert, Voivode Misić, that any Italians entering Ljubljana would be fired upon.[62]

Orlando was not prepared to go to war with Yugoslavia supported by all the other Allies. Italy had in any case no conceivable claim to Slovenia. Nor had it any to Fiume, which had not yet been effectively occupied by either side – except that its population in 1918 was at least 52 per cent Italian. As against this, there had been an equally great Yugoslav majority forty years before, and its present predominantly Italian racial composition was due primarily to the racial policies of the Hungarians, ever seeking to foster dissension among their subject peoples.[63]

Demographic calculations were really irrelevant, of course. What was at stake was simply a power struggle between Italy and the new Slav state, succeeding to the struggle between Italy and the Habsburg Empire. Nor was there any doubt that the Italians tended to regard the Yugoslavs as the heirs of Austria-Hungary. The new state comprised about 12 million people, two-thirds of whom had provided just those soldiers, sailors and airmen who had fought for the Habsburgs against Italy with the greatest resolution and ferocity. It was unfortunate that the Italians saw as natural and traditional enemies the people whom the French saw as useful Eastern allies, and the Americans saw as representatives of a principle which it pleased Washington to try to impose on European affairs.

Italy was thus in effect still at war, and still fighting for the same thing. Only the names of the enemy had changed, and different techniques had become appropriate. It was the Serbs who reached Fiume first, on 18 November, followed shortly after by the Italian commander, who immediately proposed that the Serbs should withdraw, in order to relieve international tension, on the assurance that the Italians would remain outside the city themselves. The Serbs withdrew, and Italian armoured cars and cavalry swooped in. There were certain situations for which the Italians had a flair all of their own.

The French were making this discovery in the other Adriatic ports. Thaon di Revel was simply refusing to move out of Pola or Cattaro, and at the same time seizing all the Habsburg ships which the Yugoslavs had managed to take over, hauling down the Slav flags which had been raised already, and adding these vessels to the prizes snatched beforehand by his victorious fleet. Meanwhile, Sonnino furiously accused the French of actively favouring Yugoslav interests against Italian, and General Pietro Badoglio, Diaz's deputy, compiled for his government the most comprehensive programme of techniques for destroying another state ever prepared at such short notice, for use against the Yugoslavs. Badoglio suggested in brief employing Bolshevik propaganda to separate the peasantry and workers from the middle-class nationalists; historical propaganda to remind the Serbs of 'the horrible tortures inflicted on them over the decades by the Croats'; imperialist propaganda to separate the Croats, 'still dreaming of a Great Croatia' from the 'hegemonist' Serbs; religious propaganda, especially in Bosnia-Hercegovina, to separate Orthodox from Roman Catholic, and Moslem from both; linguistic propaganda to separate the Slovenes from the rest; and monarchist propaganda to foster the concept of an independent Montenegro. These methods were to be backed up by direct action, which would take the form in those areas under Italian military control of encouraging fraternization between Italian troops and Slav women, which would indeed not have been difficult; exploiting the grievances of the now unemployed Habsburg bureaucrats; and deporting the more recalcitrant and intelligent of the clergy. Areas outside Italian military control would be attended to by squads of special agents, who would co-operate with 'the malcontented elements of the former régime'.[64] This brilliant and exhaustive recipe for destruction was immediately sanctioned by Sonnino, on 9 December. The new Yugoslav state had been proclaimed as the Kingdom of the Serbs, Croats and Slovenes only the week before. It was questionable whether it would survive another week. And now the Greeks made their contribution to tension in the Balkans. Venizelos demanded roundly on 30 December that Greece be awarded Thrace; the Dodecanese, including the islands still occupied by Italy; and Smyrna and Asia Minor, which had been promised to Italy under the terms of St Jean de Maurienne. It was an impressive bill from the nation which had contributed less to victory in material terms, calculated in either blood or treasure, than any other Allied country except Japan. The Peace Conference in Paris promised to be a memorable experience for all concerned.

4 : Balance of Power

ITALY might well have looked forward to the Peace Conference with the greatest of expectations. There were admittedly few of the Allied or Associated Powers which could not claim to have made an invaluable contribution to victory in this most closely contested of struggles. Every division had counted. But the Italians, having sacrificed proportionately more to the Entente cause in forty-one months than the British and French had in fifty-one, could argue that their contribution was unusually deserving of reward. Italy had mobilized 16 per cent of its total population for the war (more than that of any other Allied country except France) of which they had lost 16 per cent killed, as against the French 14·8 per cent, the Russian 14·6 per cent, the British 7·6 per cent, and the American 1·4 per cent. Material costs were even more impressive: Italy had expended 22 per cent of its national income on the war effort, France 14 per cent, Britain 8 per cent and the United States 2·5 per cent. Even in shipping losses, the Italians headed the field, having lost 59 per cent of their merchant fleet to enemy action, compared with losses of 43 per cent for the British and 39 per cent for the French. Italy's supply contribution had also been quite disproportionate, for a country with only 35 per cent of the productive capacity of the United Kingdom or Germany. The Italian army's complement of 7,709 cannon in 1918 compared impressively with the United Kingdom's 6,690 cannon and the 3,308 of the United States, and was exceeded on the Allied side only by the vast French park of 11,608 guns.[1] The Italian air services had expanded to a front-line fleet of 1,404 aircraft, compared with the German 2,390, the British 3,300 and the French 4,511.[2] During the war years Italian industry constructed 20,000 aircraft compared with the French production of 24,652, the German 47,637 and the Austrian output of only 5,431 aircraft and 4,346 engines.[3]

But the Peace Conference was not designed to be an equitable sharing of the spoils. Its bases for decision were French concepts of security, and the preconceptions of United States officials, neither of which were made clear at first to the people most directly affected. Wilson, who had been welcomed rapturously in Rome on 3 January 1919, made inspiring and reassuring speeches to the Italian people, but meticulously refrained from making any reference at all to the Treaty of London or the agreement of St Jean de Maurienne. His real position was made explicit on 21 January, three days after the Conference had opened, when the United States delegation affirmed that Fiume should be handed back to Yugoslavia, on the grounds that it was 'vital to the interests of the latter, and likewise assures to the more remote hinterland . . . the advantages of two competing ports . . .'[4] However, the Americans agreed that Italy should receive those parts of Istria and the Isonzo Valley essential to Italian economic interests, a compromise which would have left 75,000 Italians in Yugoslavia, but would have reduced the number of Yugoslavs consigned to Italian rule to 370,000. It could therefore legitimately be described as both 'a sane and fair-minded analysis', and 'a moderate compromise'.[5] But the Italians were not interested in a compromise: Sonnino insisted that Fiume and the ports of the Dalmatian coast were essential for Italian security. This argument has been ridiculed by Seton-Watson on the grounds that Italian naval predominance in the Adriatic could not possibly be challenged by Yugoslavia, and that the Dalmatian coast would provide Italy only with an additional military liability, not a maritime asset.[6] And this was undoubtedly true, as far as it went. But Sonnino was not just trying to strengthen Italy: his primary concern was to weaken Yugoslavia, and thereby open the Balkans to Italian exploitation – which was after all what Italy had fought for.

It soon became obvious, however, that it was not in anybody else's interests for Italy to get it. The French, who had intended to evade their commitments at St Jean de Maurienne right from the start, now joined the British in claiming that this particular undertaking had no validity, because it had not been ratified by the Russians. But nobody could be expected to believe that this was relevant either. What was relevant was that Venizelos was once again claiming Smyrna, and the British and French were disposed to let him have it, on the grounds that Greek power was less likely to complicate their imperial interests than Italian. This was not calculated to make Orlando any more conciliatory. Pointedly referring to the Croats and Slovenes as enemy people, 'against whom Italy has been fighting for four years', he demanded a frontier in Istria corresponding to the Italian concept of a 'natural' line, a frontier east of Fiume based on the principle of self-determination, and the Dalmatian coast on strategic grounds. Wilson replied with a doctrinaire challenge, asserting that the people of the United States were disgusted with the old order of strategic frontiers; that they were disgusted with the old order; and that the people of the old world also were tired of the old system, and would not put up with governments that supported it.

What Wilson had in mind was nothing less than an appeal to the Italian people over the heads of their elected representatives, just as he was later to appeal to the people of his own country, in similar fashion. The rejection of strategic frontiers could make sense only for the most powerful nation in the world, sheltered from the consequences of its rejection of European realities by 3,200 miles of water, the French army and the British fleet. Since they would be able to evade the consequences of their own acts the Americans were unconcerned that their suggestions were irresponsible, just as they were unabashed by the fact that they, who had contributed relatively less in blood and treasure to victory than any other Allied nation except Japan, were presuming to dictate terms to the nation which had contributed relatively the most.

Orlando left the Peace Conference on 24 April. Nothing had been achieved. Ten days later, Greek troops landed in Smyrna, Venizelos claiming ingeniously that they were required there to prevent the Turks from massacring Christians. His argument was called in question to some degree when the Christian Greeks promptly began massacring the Turks. This in turn gave a certain air of legality for the Italian landing in Adalia on the following day, on the grounds that such action was justified under the terms of St Jean de Maurienne, and that the order now threatened by fighting between the Greeks and Turks must be restored.[7] At the same time, 2,000 Italian soldiers left for Siberia, to show the tricolour among the Allied contingent of 60,000 Japanese, 40,000 Americans, 60,000 Czechs, 4,500 Englishmen and 1,000 French.

But Allied solidarity was becoming more remote by the minute. On 28 June the British and French formally challenged the validity of the Treaty of London, as they had already done with the St Jean de Maurienne commitments, claiming primarily that the Treaty had been nullified by subsequent events such as the withdrawal of Russia from the war and the entry of the United States into it.[8] Italy was now effectively isolated. Something had to be secured without further delay. Tittoni, who had succeeded Sonnino as Foreign Minister, reached an accord with Venizelos on the following day. Italy would support Greece in obtaining eastern and western Thrace and northern Epirus; Greece would assist Italy in obtaining the rest of Albania; Italy would receive a free zone at Smyrna for fifty years; and Italy would cede the Dodecanese to Greece, retaining however Rhodes, which would be yielded to Greece when the British yielded Cyprus. Italy would regain complete freedom of action if its demands in Asia Minor were not satisfied.

This was a substantial and apparently workable compromise between the two nations most interested in imperial expansion at the expense of Turkey. It did however depend upon the ability of the Allies to extort the appropriate concessions from Turkey, which was rendered dubious almost immediately by renewed evidence of total discord among the Allies themselves. Young Italian enthusiasts in Fiume began a series of well-organized drunken brawls with the French troops also stationed there, on the same day that Tittoni concluded his secret accord with Venizelos. Nine French soldiers had been killed and one officer wounded after a week's rioting. Then, just as the Italians were starting on the Croats, the Supreme Council of the Allies intervened, appointing a Four-Power Committee to investigate the disturbances.[9] The Committee recommended that the city should be placed under the control of a government elected by the inter-Allied Military Commission, and that it should be policed by the British or Americans.

The British were allotted the task, and agreed to move in on 12 September. Meanwhile, a supine Turkish administration agreed at Sèvres on 10 August to abandon all their former imperial possessions; to cede Thrace, Crete and most of the Aegean Islands to Greece; and to grant Smyrna and its environs autonomy under Greek administrative control. Italy was to receive only Rhodes and Castellorizzo, which it held already. Then a Three-Power Treaty signed among Britain, France and Italy on the same day secured to each a zone in Anatolia for economic exploitation.

This was a further withdrawal by Italy from the Tittoni-Venizelos compact. But the Italians had divined by now that getting anything substantial out of mainland Turkey might well be more trouble that it was worth. Tittoni began to urge upon the other Powers the importance of coming to terms with Mustapha Kemal and the provisional government in Anatolia, rather than with the lackeys who had agreed to the ruthless demands of the Treaty of Sèvres, as it was conceivable that Kemal might prove a useful ally for Italy in any future dealings with the formidably ambitious Greeks.

For the Greeks were now bent on the destruction of Turkey far more openly than the Italians had been committed to the destruction of the Yugoslav state. But then the capacity of the

Italian government to carry out any kind of policy at all was abruptly called in question when D'Annunzio seized Fiume on 10 September, two days before the British police force was due to arrive, with a Garibaldian push of a thousand fellow-adventurers, backed up by the units of the Italian army already stationed in the city, and by the crew of the battleship *Dante Alighieri,* who had mutinied the night before when ordered to leave the harbour of Fiume.

This was a very Italian way of doing things. D'Annunzio's raid was admirably in the tradition of Millo's demonstration in the Dardenelles, after his government had assured Europe that nothing of the kind would happen again. But the Fiume takeover was to have particularly serious implications for parliamentary government in Italy, at a time when successive régimes were floundering in their efforts to deal with the problems of post war economic and social dislocation, as well as with the external problems of Italy's relations with her former allies. By fortunate coincidence, however, these last began to improve immediately after D'Annunzio's coup. The Treaty of St Germain signed on 10 September conceded Italy the Brenner frontier; the French agreed on 12 September to cede to Italy a line of wells and caravan routes connecting the oases of Ghadames, Ghat and Tummo on the border between Algeria and Libya; and on 13 October Tittoni proposed the most restrained Italian suggestions so far on the question of the Yugoslav frontier. These involved the establishment of Zara and Fiume as independent cities under League control, with the area around Fiume constituting a free state; and the cession to Italy of the Istrian coast as far as Fiume, as well as the Dalmatian islands of Losinj, Vis and Palagruza. Unfortunately, however, D'Annunzio staged a plebiscite in Fiume the following week, which declared the city to be an integral part of Italy. The Americans reacted accordingly: on 13 November Wilson flatly rejected 'any solution to the problem of Fiume at variance with the one which I have advocated'; denounced D'Annunzio and his supporters as 'an imperialistic minority'; and warned the Italians that the need for 'a European adjustment is felt by all the peoples of the world, and that country which would prevent this readjustment would compel my country to take unsympathetic measures dictated solely by the irrevocable decision of the Government of my country to assist in the task of economic reconstruction only those countries which adhere to its programme.'[10]

This would certainly rank as one of the most illiterate state papers ever penned. Its implications were nevertheless sufficiently clear. The United States was prepared to use economic pressure to compel Italy to abandon even those claims which the Yugoslavs appeared to be ready to accept. Tittoni resigned, to be succeeded at the Consulta by Vittorio Scialoja. But things were improving. Wilson had already been removed from active politics by a paralytic stroke. His doctrinaire position on American participation in the League of Nations appeared certain to ensure that his nation would not in fact be able to join. It was also likely materially to assist in the defeat of his Democratic party at the next presidential elections. The British and French again began to look for a compromise with Italy, in a world in which they could count less and less upon American aid and co-operation. Clemenceau and Lloyd George agreed that Italy should have the Dalmatian islands requested by Tittoni, on condition that they should be neutralized; that Fiume and its hinterland should be made a buffer state; that the Italian proposal on Zara should be accepted; but that the Istrian coast should go to Yugoslavia. They also agreed to the division of Albania devised by Tittoni and Venizelos, with the reservation that the northern part of the little state should be opened to Yugoslav economic penetration. Further discussions among the three Powers resulted in an accord even more favourable to Italy. Lloyd George informed the Yugoslaves on 13 January that Italy should be given Fiume in return for which Yugoslavia would receive territorial compensation in the north of Albania.

The British and French modified their position again on 14 January, this time insisting that Fiume should be constituted a free state, but now insisting that unless the Yugoslavs accepted this arrangement the Treaty of London should be implemented in its entirety.[11] This solution was propounded as an ultimatum on 20 January, the Yugoslavs being given four days in which to reply. They promptly appealed to the United States, whereupon France extended the time limit by another four days. This gave the Americans time to register their protest against the unilateral action being taken by Britain and France, who continued, however, to press for Yugoslav acceptance. On 13 and 24 February Wilson flatly refused to subscribe to the Anglo-French solution, insisting nevertheless that he was prepared to accept anything agreed on by both the Yugoslavs and the Italians.

Nitti had already decided on a face-to-face approach to Belgrade, in any case. On 24 February he asked the Yugoslavs to come with him to the next session of the Peace Conference in London. Trumbić was glad to accept. The crisis was causing Yugoslavia even more distress than Italy, quite apart from the fact that every day increased the likelihood that D'Annunzio would follow up with another *coup* in the Adriatic the flood of subversion that he was directing against Belgrade from his palazzo in Fiume. Nitti took advantage of the Conference to make another attempt to frustrate Greek ambitions in the Levant, by reaffirming the importance of dealing with the provisional government of Mustapha Kemal, and of treating Turkey as 'a clearly defined national unit which should not suffer mutilation'. It was eventually agreed that annexations should be avoided, but that spheres of influence should be defined for Greece in Smyrna, for France in Cilicia and for Italy in Anatolia.[12] Meanwhile negotiations with the Yugoslavs developed to the point where at least an appearance of cordiality could be preserved when the two delegations met on 11 May at the Villa Casanova in Pallanza. But the Nitti-Tittoni régime fell before any definite agreement could be reached on any of the points at issue. Old Giolitti, cool and cruel, as perceptive of historical movements as he was indifferent to their effects, succeeded as Prime Minister, bringing with him to the Consulta the congenially realistic trimmer Carlo Sforza.

They had more than enough opportunity for their particular talents. D'Annunzio's private navy was stopping Italian ships on the high seas and forcing them to disgorge cargoes of foodstuffs in Fiume to keep the city supplied. And now the infection of mutiny was spreading. A regiment had disobeyed when ordered to sail for Valona. The entire hinterland of Libya was in revolt. It was time for Italy to cut its losses, a thing which, fortunately, Giolitti never found it difficult to do. An occasion was provided by the decision of the French on 15 June to award to Albania the strategic position of Koritzia, in the northern Epirus, and a month later Giolitti told the Senate that he wanted to see Albania completely independent of all foreign control. Negotiations were immediately initiated with the régime in Tirana. The Italian and Albanian governments agreed on 2 August that all Italian forces should be withdrawn immediately, and that Italy should retain only the island of Saseno, off the coast of Valona. It so happened that details of the Tittoni-Venizelos accord were printed in the Greek press for the first time on 5 August, and on the following day Sforza had the pleasure of denouncing it in Parliament, affirming that the friendship of Albania was of more value to Italy than the retention of Valona.[13] He also expressed the view that Russia should be left to work out its own destiny without foreign interference, announcing that representatives were being exchanged between Rome and Moscow to reach an agreement between the two nations. As for Turkey, Italy wished to offer to 'the Turks of Anatolia . . . cordial, loyal co-operation, both economic and moral, which will leave intact both the liberty and the sovereignty of Turkey'.[14]

This was a masterstroke. By endorsing the independence of Albania, the Italians called a check to the territorial ambitions of both Greece in the south and Yugoslavia in the north. by espousing co-operation with Turkey, they exposed the Greeks as rapacious imperialistic aggressors. Nor had anything really been lost. The occupants of Saseno neutralized Albania in the meantime, and provided a springboard for future occupation of the country when this should become practicable. That they had abandoned an empire in Anatolia was far more serious, but this could be compensated for by the fact that the Greeks would now be left on their own to withstand the full fury of Turkish nationalism.[15] The diplomatic benefits of this were immediately noticeable. Time was completely on the Italians' side: nobody was prepared to help an apparently intransigent Yugoslavia against a seemingly conciliatory Italy; nor was Wilson available any longer to discourage the British and French from applying persuasion to Belgrade. The Yugoslavs found themselves completely abandoned. The British and French positively supported the Italians in securing the Trumbić-Bertolini Agreement of 5 September 1920, under which Italy acquired 680,000 tons of the original Habsburg merchant fleet, and Yugoslavia only 117,000 tons. Then on 21 September French Foreign Minister Millerand briskly reminded Belgrade that 'the French Government attaches great importance to the prompt and satisfactory conclusion of the Adriatic question . . . [and] it is desirable that the government in Belgrade . . . approach with the desire of reaching a speedy agreement . . .'.[16]

Belgrade accepted what it could not avoid, and on 12 November Sforza and Trumbić signed the Treaty of Rapallo. By the terms of this Italy got all of northern Istria, up to Mount Nevoso, reaching at most points beyond the limits of the Treaty of London line, to ingest a further 100,000 Yugoslavs; Zara became an Italian enclave in Dalmatia, as did the island groups of Cherso, Lussin, Lagosta and Pelagosa; Fiume became independent 'in perpetuity'; and linguistic and economic rights were assured to the 10,000 Italians remaining in Yugoslav Dalmatia, and also to the 16,000 Slavs in Fiume and Zara, but not to the other 470,000 Slavs now within the Italian frontier.

The arrangement was hardly a triumph of the principle of ethnic self-determination. But it was no less so than any of the other experiments in redefining the boundaries of Europe. Italy had recovered 700,000 Italians from Austrian rule, and taken 230,000 Germans and 470,000 Slavs to go with them. Romania by comparison had acquired 1,500,000 Magyars, 250,000 Germans and 80,000 Serbs; Poland engulfed 4 million Russians, 1 million Germans and 500,000 Lithuanians; and Yugoslavia itself had ingested 500,000 Germans, 467,000 Magyars, 440,000 Albanians and 231,000 Romanians, to mention only the minority groups, and disregarding the 4 million Croats and Slovenes yoked unwillingly to the Serb master race.[17] Czechoslovakia could certainly be termed a congeries of minorities rather than a nation, with 6·5 million Czechs attempting to dominate 3·1 million Germans, 2 million Slovaks, 700,000 Magyars, 600,000 Ukranians and 200,000 Poles. Valid comparisons are of course scarcely possible, but one would at least be entitled to argue that the American-inspired frontier changes in European after 1918 had extended the area of oppression rather than narrowed it. Italy had at least not suppressed more people than it liberated.

In territorial terms, the paucity of Italy's reward was astonishing. The British and French had of course done best. Counting its mandated territories, the British Empire had increased in size by 2·3 million square miles, and in population by 28 millions; while the French Empire had similarly swelled by an addition of 2·7 million square miles and 19 million subjects.[18] Romania, whose losses in killed and wounded were about a quarter those of Italy, and whose financial expenditure was less than one-eighth, was recompensed with 68,790 square miles of territory, with 9,389,000 inhabitants. Italy's total territorial gain was 23,726 square miles, and its population gain 1,672,000.[19]

D'Annunzio was not prepared to accept this compromise without a protest. Admiral Millo, the raider of the Dardanelles, meeting with him at sea on 16 November, attempted to persuade him to make his peace with the government in Rome. D'Annunzio's reply, having secured the loyalty of two torpedo-boats, was to declare war on Italy on 1 December. But on 28 December troops under General Caviglia bombarded Fiume, whereupon D'Annunzio, realizing the futility of his venture, released his supporters from their oaths of fealty to him on the following day, and Caviglia marched his troops into the city on 18 January.

Relieved of the Fiume embarrassment, Sforza could now turn all his attention to Turkey. The isolation of Greece was completed in London on 24 January 1921. Sforza persuaded the British and French to recognize the government of Mustapha Kemal, in return for promises of economic opportunities in Anatolia. The Italians moreover undertook to assist the Ankara government in seeking the revision of the Treaty of Sèvres, with particular reference to those areas being claimed by the Greeks. Ankara's response was to renew their offensive in Anatolia. The spectacle of the Greeks pressing on aggressively to disaster could only be be gratifying to the Italians, who gained another conciliatory triumph when their solution to the Anglo-French dispute over the Silesian frontier was eventually accepted in large measure. But Sforza's efforts as peacemaker backfired when he announced on 25 June that he had agreed to let the Yugoslavs have the economically unimportant coastline between Fiume and its joint city, Susak. The territory was immediately seized and incorporated in Fiume by some of D'Annunzio's *arditi,* still hanging around after their leader had left, and Giolitti and Sforza resigned office, after having worked as perceptively for the kingdom as any Italian politicians since Venosta.

Italian extremists might not be happy with what their parliamentary régime was achieving, but Sforza and Giolitti had managed to secure a large measure of immensely valuable support from Britain and France, instead of the resolute hostility which Sonnino had had to bear. This altered relationship proved immediately helpful. Yugoslav irregulars were pressing again upon the northern frontier of Albania, and the Greeks, in the full tide of imperialist enthusiasm, were beginning to protest about the alleged activities of Albanian bandits in the Epirus. A Yugoslav-fomented tribal rebellion broke out in the north in November. The British brought the matter before a Conference of Ambassadors, which on 9 November set up a commission to delimit the frontiers of the strategically situated little state, noting in particular that the violation of Albania's defined boundaries or a threat to its independence would constitute a menace to

Italy. This was followed up, again on British instigation, by a formal demand that Yugoslavia withdraw its forces from northern Albania.

Events continued to run Italy's way in the Middle East. On 27 July 1922 the Greeks announced their intention of occupying Constantinople. Three weeks later, fighting between the Greek invaders and the Turkish nationalists began again in Anatolia, and by 26 August it had developed into a major Turkish offensive. A fortnight later the Greeks were in headlong flight for Smyrna, totally defeated. Quick to grasp the opportunity, the Italian government denounced the clauses of the Treaty of Sèvres which had ceded the Dodecanese Islands to Greece, on the grounds that the Treaty was now clearly inoperative. It had been a good year for Italy. Yugoslavia had been pressured into giving up another 100,000 inhabitants and was about to be cheated out of Fiume; Albania had virtually had its frontiers guaranteed by all the Great Powers; and Greek ambitions in the eastern Mediterranean had collapsed in calamitous defeat.

It was not enough to save the parliamentary régime in Italy, for even its external successes now looked too much like the successes of weakness, and its efforts to deal with the problems of post-war reconstruction could only be termed inadequate. It was true that Italian industry had performed impressively during the war years: production of iron and steel had both increased by nearly 50 per cent, from 706,000 tons to 1 million tons, and from 911,000 tons to 1,332,000 tons, respectively,[20] whereas German production had remained virtually static during that period, and Austrian iron output had fallen by 36 per cent.[21] But Italy was still poorer after the war, by comparison with its Allies, than it had been before. The value of the lira had fallen from eighty-one gold centismo in 1918, to only eighteen centismo by the end of 1920.[22] By March 1920,[23] bread support prices were costing the exchequer 500 million lire a month, largely because wheat production had fallen to 37 million quintals from the pre-war peak of 51 millions in 1911–13.[24] Emigration swelled from 253,000 in 1919 to 615,000 in 1920 – but this avenue of escape was sub-

5a. Gabriele d'Annunzio 1863–1938
Radio Times Hulton Picture Library

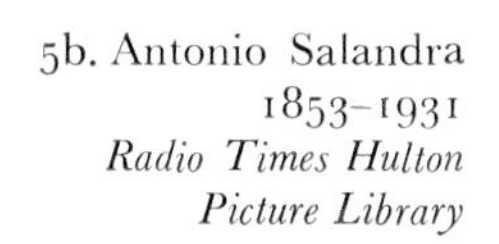

5b. Antonio Salandra 1853–1931
Radio Times Hulton Picture Library

6a. Count Luigi Cadorna 1850–1928
Radio Times Hulton Picture Library

6b. Giovanni Giolitti 1842–1928
Radio Times Hulton Picture Library

stantially restricted by the action of the United States in imposing a quota of 40,000 for Italian immigration after 1921.

Although by the middle of 1921 there was some economic recovery apparent, two factors prevented the alleviation of social distress from preserving the parliamentary régime. One was the evident instability of the régime itself – Italy suffered six different governments between 1919 and 1922. Orlando fell in June 1919; Nitti lasted from June 1919 to June 1920; Giolitti's fifth premiership took him to the following June. Then Bonomi held office until February 1922; Facta hung on for the next eight months, and he was succeeded by Mussolini in October. There were two major consequences of this continuing tumult of changing ministries. In the first place, it unquestionably weakened Italy's posture in international conferences: Italian representatives found themselves frequently without a government to instruct them at all, and normally without a government secure enough to formulate a lasting policy. In the second, it encouraged succeeding Italian prime ministers to disregard Parliament entirely, and to rule as far as possible by decree, relying on the civil service to carry on the government of the country.[25]

This was the second and ultimately disastrous factor. A parliamentary régime can sometimes survive brilliantly by using such methods, as the men of the Fourth Republic succeeded in doing in France. But the French could rely on the services of the most intelligent and prestigious bureaucracy in Europe. The Italian civil service of the post-war period had no such claims to distinction. And government by decree is a desperate game for parliamentarians to play, even in ideal circumstances, simply because it involves, in the last resort, a reliance on force rather than electoral approval, thereby challenging precisely those dissident elements which foster parliamentary instability, whose methods it employs. Revolutionaries are liable to know more about the uses of force than the establishment, and they are certainly likely to be happier in making use of it.

Italy was swept by bloodstained anarchy throughout the whole period. Waves of general strikes and proletarian protest demonstrations precipitated battles with the police, causing 320 deaths between April 1919 and September 1920. Bloodshed increased when counter-revolutionary groups, particularly the *fascisti,* took a hand against the strikers. On 21 November 1920 ten people were killed by bomb or bullet in Bologna; the displacement of D'Annunzio from Fiume cost fifty-three lives; at least 176 people were murdered in the five weeks before, and two weeks after the election of 1921; and seventy-four more political murders occurred between 15 August and 22 September.[26]

There was nothing really very extraordinary about all this. Mercifully fewer attempts have been made to explain Mussolini's Fascism in terms of Italian history and psychology, than to interpret Hitler's Nazism in terms of German national personality. Analyses of either are irrelevant. There was nothing remarkable about what happened in Italy in 1922 and in Germany ten years later. Authoritarian, non-Communist revolutionary movements manifested themselves in the inter-war period in every continent and almost every country in the world. By 1940, they flourished in China, Japan, throughout almost all of the Americas, in independent Africa and the Middle East, and in all of central, eastern and southern Europe. The truly aberrant features of the global political scene, in the inter-war as in the post-war years, were the parliamentary democracies. It was not remarkable that millions of ex-soldiers, unsettled by war and dissatisfied with the peacetime world to which they returned, should be disposed to introduce into civilian political life their wartime practices of anarchy and violence; it was not surprising that the very success of the Communist revolution in Russia should precipitate the formation of counter-revolutionary action groups outside Russia, among all those who rejected Communism, at the same time as it encouraged the very kind of left-wing activities that would give these action groups a sanction and an opportunity for violence; it was nothing to wonder at that men who had spent the past four years in a pressurized atmosphere of discipline and patriotic slogans should embrace the principles of leadership and nationalism thereafter. Nor was it surprising that even lifelong civilians should be prepared to accept any alternative to a parliamentary régime which did not appear to be capable of dealing with the two most urgent of all human problems, hunger and unemployment.

Mussolini's ascent to office was thus a natural event in the Italy of his time, and was recognized as such by his contemporaries. It did not involve any greater change in the direction of Italian policies than did the accession of Charles de Gaulle in France in 1958. What had taken place was in essence a bloodless constitutional change. A system which appeared to foster instability had been discarded in favour of one which promised stability. A charismatic leader had been accepted in preference to a parliament which in many respects appeared to be incapable of governing.

Mussolini's primary task in foreign affairs was in fact the same as de Gaulle's: to affirm the importance and authority of his nation to a world which had ceased to take it seriously. The first challenge to be met was that of France. On 8 November 1921 the French government had announced that all children born in Tunis, one of whose parents had also been born there, were *ipso facto* French subjects; they had also, at the Washington Conference, contested Italian claims to naval parity with France. Mussolini approached the problem of Italy's status in the world outside at once. In his first speech to the Chamber of Deputies after assuming office, he affirmed:

> 'My formula is simple – *niente per niente.* Those who wish to have concrete proofs of friendship from us must give us concrete proofs of friendship in return. . . . Rome stands in line with Paris and London, but Italy must undertake and compel her Allies to undertake a courageous and severe examination of the realities of the situation. . . . Does an Entente still exist in the real meaning of the word? . . . What is the position of Italy in this Entente, of Italy which, by the weakness of its Governments, has lost strong positions in the

> Adriatic and the Mediterranean, while indulging in long debates on her fundamental rights. . . .'[27]

Mussolini's first attempts to compel the Western Powers to undertake this examination of conscience may politely be termed symbolic. On 11 October an armistice had been arranged between Greece and nationalist Turkey, terms of peace for which were to be discussed by the Powers on 20 November at Lausanne. Mussolini left Rome on 17 November for the Conference, but halted his trip at Territet, a few miles nearer Italy than Lausanne,[28] thus compelling Poincaré and Curzon to come to meet him for a pre-Conference discussion. This achieved at least a recognition of Italy's equal status with Britain and France in the official communique, even though this statement necessarily implied that Italy had not been exactly equal before. The Conference was not, however, immediately followed up by any concrete results, as Mussolini had envisaged. He succeeded only in irritating the British by demanding that Italy should retain the Dodecanese, and in clashing with the French on the question of German reparation payments. Italy then sided with France against Britain in declaring Germany in default at the meeting of the Reparations Commission on 9 January 1923, although Mussolini affirmed that an understanding on the reparations question 'can only be arrived at with the participation and consent of England'; insisted that the French occupation of the Ruhr should be solely of a military character; and claimed that Italian engineers had accompanied the invading Franco-Belgian armies on 11 January, only because 'Italy, which has no coal, cannot afford the luxury of renunciation or isolation. . . .'[29]

This was all a trifle incoherent, but it was not without its good effects. Paris and London were both prepared to put up with a reasonable amount of intimidation and equivocation for the sake of having a government in Rome which could at least count on support from its own people for whatever policies it decided to carry out. The British in particular were prepared to welcome almost any continental rival to the overweening predominance of France in Europe. They accordingly accepted on 4 February Mussolini's demand that Italian sovereignty over the Dodecanese should be recognized. Not that it was a great concession. France had allotted to itself the mandate for Syria, and Britain had done the same in respect to Palestine and Transjordania, as well as retaining a dominating position in Egypt and holding firm to Cyprus. Italian presence in the eastern Mediterranean might pose some kind of threat to British and French influence in that region, but it would have been difficult to contest the Italian claims except on the principle that Italy's contributions to the cause of the Entente in the war entitled it to as little reward as possible afterwards, and this would hardly have been a rational policy for London to follow. On 7 May King George V paid a state visit to Rome, presenting Mussolini with the Order of the Bath. He was followed by the Prime Minister of Hungary, then by Polish and Austrian and later Romanian representatives. On 24 July the Treaty of Lausanne confirmed absolutely Italian sovereignty over the Dodecanese. All this of course was to have been expected. Nobody doubted that Italy was the most important Power east of the Rhine – but neither could anybody doubt that there was in reality only one Power worthy of the name in continental Europe, and that was France. Italy could not challenge France either militarily or economically, and could only continue to hold second place for as long as Germany remained disarmed and diplomatically impotent. There seemed no reason why any small nation should be concerned to bid for Italian protection or forbearance so long as it could obtain the support of France. But fortune was about to give Mussolini the opportunity to show that French support could not always be counted on.

The Inter-Allied Commission appointed by the Conference of Ambassadors to define the frontiers of Albania had just finished their work in the north of that country. Three cars left the Greek town of Janina on the morning of 28 August, carrying the commissioners to the scene of their labours in the southern frontier area. The first car brought Albanian officials; the second the

Italian General Tellini, the chairman of the Commission, two other Italian officers, an Italian chauffeur and an Albanian interpreter; and the third the Greek officials. The Albanians reached their destination safely; the Greeks arrived two hours later, with the explanation that they had been delayed by engine failure; the car carrying the Italians was stopped by a road block and all five occupants shot dead.

There was no immediate indication as to who the assassins were, or what were their motives. Any chances of ever finding out were materially diminished by the action of the Greek officials in the third car, who had burnt the trees used to form the road block when they cleared it away after arriving at the scene of the crime.[30] The Italian Ambassador in Athens, Montagna, immediately demanded that the Greek government take proper steps at once to arrest and convict the assassins, following up rather prematurely with the suggestion that the assassins had in fact been subsidized by the Greek government. Meanwhile, Thaon di Revel's ships had put to sea again. An ultimatum was delivered by Mussolini to the Greek government on 29 August, along lines clearly inspired by the Austrian ultimatum to Belgrade after the Sarajevo affair. Its more cogent demands were that an enquiry should be carried out within five days, with the assistance of the Italian military attaché; that all persons found guilty should be sentenced to death; that the Greek government should pay Italy an indemnity of 50 million lire; and that a reply should be received within twenty-four hours.

The Greek reply was that the demands constituted an outrage to the honour and a violation of the sovereignty of the Greek state. However, the Greeks were not too intransigent. They offered to accept any helpful information from the Italian military attaché; and to pay 'an equitable indemnity to the families of the victims'.[31] They also informed the Italians that:

> 'If, contrary to expectation, the Italian Government were unwilling to recognise the satisfaction given as adequate, the Hellenic Government has the honour to inform the Royal

Italian Legation that, in accordance with the provision of the Covenant of the League of Nations, it will appeal to the League and undertake to accept its decisions.'[32]

If Italy was acting like Austria, then Greece was acting like Serbia.[33] But the Italians had a capacity for ready action not available to the Habsburgs. Mussolini replied on 31 August, asserting that 'the crime was of a political character, and was therefore certainly committed by Greeks'; that the response of the Greek government 'must be considered . . . as a refusal of the essential reparation for the crime that has been committed'; and that accordingly such an 'unjustifiable attitude compels the Italian government to recall the Greek government to a sense of its responsibility'.[34] It is doubtful if any government of a sovereign state had ever referred to another similar government in modern times in quite such a tone of patronizing contempt. The means for carrying out the chastisement were ready at hand. Mussolini had already been considering adding Corfu to his Dodecanese acquisitions.[35] A squadron commanded by Admiral Solari appeared off the island on the same day, but unfortunately, the enthusiastic Italian commander exceeded his instructions. Mussolini had ordered that the Greeks be given two hours in order to surrender; they actually got thirty minutes. The Italian fleet then opened fire, killing sixteen people and wounding another fifty.

Even Mussolini admitted that this was a bad start. But the incident in effect developed in a manner particularly gratifying to Italy. The Greeks had already appealed to the Council of the League, whereupon the competence of the Council to deal with the situation at all was challenged by the Italian representative, Salandra, on the grounds that the Conference of Ambassadors had itself begun to investigate the Janina murders. The authority of the Council was backed by the British representative, Cecil, in answer to which Mussolini intervened personally on 4 September, deploring the profoundly wounding attitude of the British; denying the competence of the League to concern itself with a matter in which no element of risk of war was involved, and which even more importantly concerned Italian honour; and warning that he would disregard the authority of the Council if it attempted to interfere.[36]

It is extremely probable that Mussolini was genuinely surprised that the Council should have shown any interest. He was undoubtedly simply not aware of either the functions or the pretensions of the international body; neither for that matter was he fully informed about his own constitutional position in Italy, for on 11 August he had spoken of 'my government', seemingly not realizing that only the king as Head of State was entitled to use the possessive term. His disdain for the League was in any event quite appropriate, as the organization had no capacity to interfere in police actions by Great Powers, unless other Great Powers considered the matter sufficiently in their interests to be worth fighting for. And the European Great Powers did not think so in this instance. Poincaré had taken steps to insure that a solution would be found in the Conference of Ambassadors, which would be sympathetic to the Italian case, because it was after all officials from that body who had been assassinated. Curzon hastened to assure the Italians that Cecil's condemnations in the Council should not be taken too seriously, and warned the British Cabinet that the Treasury was appalled at the thought of even contemplating economic sanctions against Italy. Nor was there any question of sterner measures. At that time the British Mediterranean fleet, except for two battleships and five destroyers, was on a watching brief in the Near East, and units were being moved from the vicinity of the Dodecanese to Corfu.[37] This inspired Thaon di Revel to do some strategic arithmetic.

On 20 September he assured Mussolini that Italy would be able to cope with a British challenge so long as it could deploy 200 aircraft, as the British had only 120 on their carriers.[38] The fact was however, that for all the talk of Fascist wings darkening the sky,[39] which had been current earlier in the year,[40] there were only sixty-six first-line fighting aircraft ready for action in all of Italy.[41] But they were not going to be needed. The Committee of Enquiry appointed by the Conference of Ambassadors reported on 22 September that 'the enquiry carried out by the Hellenic authorities after the crime certainly shows cases of negligence on the part of those authorities . . .'. The Ambassadors themselves increased the pressure on Greece substantially on the following day by requiring that the Greeks would have to provide positive proof that they had not committed any negligences: they were in other words guilty until proved innocent. Paul Cambon adduced on 24 September as a proof of Greek negligence the fact that Athens had so far not sacked a single official remotely connected with the case. The Ambassadors accordingly resolved on 26 September that the indemnity of 50 million lire should in fact be paid to Italy, noting that the Italian government had promised to evacuate Corfu on 27 September. The Italians duly sailed away on the following day, returning immediately when the Greeks began to temporize about the payment. Athens responded appropriately; the indemnity was paid; and the Italian fleet finally left Corfu harbour on 29 September, not to return for twelve more years.

Boldness had won. Martin Gilbert has characterized the Italian actions as hasty, unnecessary and murderous,[42] but there had been excellent precedents for them, as Mussolini pointed out, and their consequences were wholly beneficial for Italy. The main goal, however, had been reached, in that the subordinate status of Greece in the eastern Mediterranean had been confirmed. A Commission of Jurists appointed by the Council to determine its legal position *ex post facto* effectively supported the Italian position by concluding that the Council must refuse to accept an application for arbitration 'where such a dispute already forms the subject of arbitration or of judicial proceedings . . .'.[43] All that Mussolini really had to fear was that Italy's resort to traditional methods of power politics might have frightened the Balkan states into closer alignments with France. A treaty between Czechoslovakia and France was in fact discussed in October 1923, immediately after the Corfu affair. It was followed up by offers from France of credits to Yugoslavia, Romania and Poland to buy French munitions and military equipment.

The isolation of Italy was expected to be completed at the Conference of the Little Entente (Czechoslovakia, Yugoslavia and Romania) scheduled to be held in Belgrade on 10 January 1924. But it was the opposite that happened – Italy became the most sought-after nation in Europe. When the Fascist Prime Minister Primo de Rivera, who had seized power on 15 September 1923, accompanied the King and Queen of Spain on a visit to Rome, on 19 November, he was introduced by the Spanish sovereign as 'my Mussolini'. On 30 November, Mussolini announced that a commercial treaty with Russia was in train, involving the *de jure* recognition of the Communist régime. A commercial treaty with Albania was concluded on 21 January, and diplomatic relations with Greece were restored two days later. Most importantly, a Treaty of Friendship and Co-operation with Yugoslavia was signed on 27 January, pledging the two countries to assist each other politically and diplomatically in the event of an unprovoked attack, and recognizing 'the full and complete sovereignty of the Kingdom of Italy over the city and port of Fiume'.[44] The Treaty with Russia was signed at last on 8 February. Discussions on a further treaty of friendship and co-operation with Czechoslovakia were begun on 15 May, due to the initiative of the Czech Prime Minister. This flood of diplomatic activity was even carried into the work of the League of Nations. Mussolini complacently told the Deputies on 11 November that 'reactionary Italy' had so far signed twelve conventions, Britain seven, Belgium four and France and Germany none.[45] Meanwhile, remaining colonial difficulties were congenially ironed out. Badoglio's reconquest of Libya made substantial progress with the occupation of Mizda and Syrte, and on 15 July the British at last agreed to concede Jubaland to Italy's east African empire.

While Italian prestige continued to rise, between 8 and 13 December 1924 the League of Nations deliberated in Rome. Discussions followed among the British, Italians and French on the question of a series of frontier guarantees consequent upon

Germany's admission to the League of Nations. Britain and Italy found themselves in accord again against France, in advocating a five-Power rather than tripartite arrangement, and in agreeing that frontier guarantees should not be extended to Poland or Czechoslovakia. Meanwhile, a massive series of financial, legal and political agreements were reached with Yugoslavia under the general title of the Nettuno Accords of 21 July; a Commercial Treaty with Hungary was concluded on 5 September; and on 16 October it was agreed at Locarno that Italy and Britain would guarantee the existing frontiers of Germany, Belgium and France. This was followed by a Commercial Treaty between Italy and Germany on 31 October, the first to be signed by post-war Germany with any of the Great Powers. Then on 5 December an accord was reached with the Egyptian government on the definition of its frontier with Libya, Italy receiving the oasis of Giarabub in return for the Bay of Sollum. Agreement was even reached with the British on their relations with Abyssinia, which had been admitted to the League of Nations with Italian sponsorship on 28 September 1923. The British now agreed to recognize an exclusive Italian economic interest in the west of Abyssinia, in the event of Britain's receiving the desired concession from the Abyssinians on Lake Tana.

This was not exactly a free hand from the British to partition Abyssinia, although it undoubtedly showed a readiness on the part of the British to disregard whatever interest the Abyssinians may have had in the future of their own country. There was no denying that Anglo-Italian relations were reaching ever new levels of cordiality. So indeed were Yugoslav-Italian relations. Nincic of Yugoslavia visited Rome in February, to discuss the possibility of a tripartite agreement between his country, Italy and France. The Greeks and Poles followed. Italian prestige was enhanced still further by a petulant outburst by the Bavarian Prime Minister referring to the 'brutal excesses' being perpetrated by the Italian authorities against the German minority in the Trentino, and proposing to free the Germans in the Alto Adige, 'as far as we are able'. Mussolini in reply jovially ridiculed the cultural pretensions of the Germans, and their ignorance of Italy; declared that Italian policy would not deflect one inch; and promised rhetorically that, if necessary, Fascist Italy would carry its flag still further than the Brenner Pass, 'but strike it, never!'.[46]

The implication that Italy might under some circumstances find it appropriate to invade Austria naturally evoked further criticism from the Austrian Chancellor, who was thereupon required by Mussolini to explain his words.[47] It was all naturally gratifying to the French: the Paris Press congratulated Mussolini on knowing how to talk to the Germans. Mussolini replied by suggesting that a Franco-Italian bloc of 80 millions could counterbalance the Germans and thereby impose peace.[48] But prospects of such an accord were positively diminishing with the triumphant progress of Italian diplomacy. Mussolini had taken the occasion of his visit to newly pacified Libya to proclaim that the Italians 'were a Mediterranean people'. His flamboyant air force general, Italo Balbo, dramatically flew to Tunisia four days later, where an Italian majority of 120,000 was still being painfully incorporated by a French minority of some 91,178. Lloyd George in England rapturously hailed Italian challenges to French hegemony in the Mediterranean by suggesting that the human race should be grateful if Italy somehow acquired all the former colonial territories abandoned by the Turks. The French however ostentatiously began naval exercises off the coast of Libya, which drew from Mussolini the warning that Fascist Italy possessed 'unlimited forces and immeasurable spiritual strength'.[49]

Sparring of this kind never hurt anybody. What had far more serious implications was the sudden recrudescence of Italian-Yugoslav rivalry in the Balkans. The issue naturally was Albania, where Ahmed Zogu had established himself as dictator with Yugoslav help, but had since decided that Italian friendship could be more rewarding than that of Belgrade. In June 1926 the Yugoslavs denounced the Nettuno Accords, alleging with complete justification continued subversive Italian intrigues in Dalmatia. For the moment, Mussolini contented himself with completing Treaties of Friendship, Conciliation and Neutrality with Spain on 7 August and with Italy's other Latin partner, Romania, on 16 September. Then on 27 November the Treaty of Tirana was signed, stating that 'any disturbance threatening the political, legal and territorial *status quo* of Albania is contrary to their common interests'; and guaranteed that neither Italy nor Albania should 'conclude with other Powers any political or military agreements prejudicial to the interests of the other party . . .'.[50] In return, Zogu received a grant of 50 million gold francs from Italy, for his personal bank account.

The treaty was naturally denounced in Belgrade as effectively constituting an Italian protectorate over Albania. There was no doubt that Rome had been applying pressure on Tirana to that end ever since June, nor was there any doubt that Zogu had become in the most complete sense Mussolini's client. The entire Yugoslav cabinet resigned in protest against this subordination of a Balkan state. The French followed, criticizing Italian pretensions to a Balkan hegemony, to which the *Giornale d'Italia* irritably replied that France was always in the forefront of resistance to Italian policies, and made it necessary for Italy to remain in a permanent state of war.[51] The more effective response, however, was the conclusion of a Treaty of Conciliation and Arbitration with Germany, the first of its kind, on 22 December, in the discussions on which Mussolini led the Germans to believe that Italy would not necessarily oppose an *Anschluss* between Germany and Austria. The only remaining point of dispute with Britain was removed with an Anglo-Italian Agreement on the Red Sea littoral on 7 February. The way was now clear in the Balkans.

Material weakness had hitherto lent an unreal quality to any Italian pretensions to rivalry with France. Now in 1927 Italy possessed the third largest army and probably second largest air force in the world, as well as a navy marginally larger than that of France.[52] And not only that, Italian aviation technology had proved itself among the best in the world: a Macchi 17 had won the Schneider Trophy for air speed as early as 1917. In 1924 the Marchese di Pinedo had established a long-distance record, by flying 20,000 miles to Tokyo, extending this by a further 14,000 miles in the following year. Mario Bernhardi won the Schneider Cup again for Italy in 1926, in a Macchi M39, with a speed of 246 m.p.h., and in the same year, Umberto Nobile successfully piloted the Amundsen expedition over the North Pole in the Italian-designed airship *Norge,* and Caproni developed his Ca6000 triplane into the biggest landplane in the world, with six motors and over 3,000 h.p. Then in 1927 the Schneider Cup was won yet again by a Macchi M52. The military benefits of these technological achievements were already apparent. Italy's best fighter, the Fiat CR20, with a top speed of 171 m.p.h., was nine m.p.h. faster than France's Dewotine De9, and 62 m.p.h. faster than Britain's Hawker Hyderabad. Italian productive capacity had also increased considerably. Italian shipyards built 101,000 tons of merchant shipping in 1926, compared with only 20,000 tons in 1915.[53] Industrial production had increased by 30 per cent in the same period; production of pig iron by a similar percentage, from 750,000 tons to 1,100,000; and steel production by over 100 per cent, from 1 million to 2·1 million tons.[54] The improvement was noteworthy, even in relative terms. Italy produced 3·85 per cent as much iron as Germany in 1915, and 8·2 per cent as much steel. Relative figures in 1927 were 7·7 and 13 per cent.

Although these achievements did not alter Italy's position in the hierarchy of world Powers, what they did do, apparently, was to make it easier for it to sustain that position. Now, for the first time, Franco-Italian rivalry became almost reasonable – it could at least become open. Mussolini rejected an invitation to attend a further Naval Disarmament Conference in Washington in February; denounced alleged military preparations by Yugoslavia on 18 March; and on 26 May called for a great programme of aerial rearmament, with 'Fascist wings to darken the face of the sun', after a campaign in the official Fascist Press against the magnitude of French military spending. A Treaty of Friendship and Arbitration was concluded with the Hungarian dictatorship, and arms were smuggled across the border from Italy to equip the Fascists of Austria, just as they had been smuggled for years past to equip the separatists of Croatia and Slovenia. The Yugoslavs attempted to preserve their position by breaking off diplomatic relations with Albania on 12 June, and by concluding a Treaty of Friendship and Arbitration with France on 11 November. French Foreign Minister Briand attempted to avoid the appearance of a confrontation with Italy by asking Mussolini to participate. But it had never been any part of Italian policy to avoid the appearance of a confrontation with the Slavs. A twenty-year defensive alliance was concluded eleven days later between Italy and Albania, effectively guaranteeing Italian control over the little country's security forces.

This was the beginning of the Italian predominance. The past decade had been spent in establishing Italy's claim to recognition by powerful and neglectful Allies. For most of the next ten years Italy was to appear as the Great European Power, alone possessed of strength to act and will to make that strength effective. The real tragedy of the 1930s was that the Western Powers failed to recognize in the apparent disturber of world peace its only available guarantor.

For the Italian net now swept over the Balkans. Hungary was virtually dependent on Italy for its supplies of military equipment; Turkey signed a Treaty of Friendship and Co-operation in February; Greece did likewise in September, and Italy's hold over it was strengthened in July 1929, when Mussolini visited King Boris of Bulgaria, encouraging him in his nationalist designs on Greek-occupied Thrace. Friendless Bulgaria was an easy conquest: the Italians had acquired a free hand at Varna and a virtual monopoly of the small Bulgarian market for motor vehicles by October 1930, when dynastic ties between the two nations were established by Boris's marriage with the Princess Giovanna of Savoy.

The initiative had been taken away from the French entirely. Albania was an Italian protectorate; Bulgaria a dynastic and economic partner; Greece and Turkey apparently reconciled by Italian mediation and too suspicious of each other and of Bulgaria to be capable of opposing Italian plans; Hungary a military client state; and Romania an increasingly convincing imitation of the cruder aspects of Italian Fascism. That left Yugoslavia, and Yugoslavia's existence as a viable nation had become more vulnerable than ever since King Alexander had established a royal dictatorship in January 1929, and had been devoting himself to crushing every manifestation of minority sentiment in his multi-racial and multi-religious kingdom. Even Serb traditions were suffering from this attempt to create a new Slav unity, but as the King's policies were drafted by Serb ministers and implemented by Serb police, the Croats and Slovenes were suffering far worse. In January the Italians began actively training Croat separatists for a coup against Alexander. Relations between the two Fascist movements became closer after Mussolini took personal charge of Italian foreign affairs in July. It was an appropriate move, for it showed the world that economic distress was fostering the emergence of Fascism throughout central and eastern Europe. On 31 July the Nazis received 37·3 per cent of the votes cast in elections in Germany, after a campaign in which 250 people had been killed. General Gombos, former Minister of War and an avowed admirer of Italian Fascism, came to power as Prime Minister in Hungary on 30 September, while in Albania Zogu, now calling himself King Zog I, clamped his royal dictatorship tighter by arresting 200 alleged dissidents, seven of whom were sentenced to death. A treaty binding the economies of Italy and Hungary still more closely was drafted after a visit by Gombos to Rome on 8 November, during which the Hungarian leader claimed that 'friendship with Italy was the unalterable pole of Hungarian foreign policy'.[56] While Balbo ridiculed the idea of anybody taking the League of Nations seriously,[57] Mussolini confidently flouted the idea of a Four-Power Pact among the great European states, to establish a directorate of European affairs which would at once preserve peace, rationalize the position of Germany, and provide Italy with a forum in which it could always count upon support against France from either the British or Germans.[58]

There were of course certain obstacles to this, one of which was the extraordinary refusal of Yugoslavia to fall apart, despite the worst economic crisis in Europe.[59] A raid by Croat separatists out of Zara into the region of Lika in November was routed by the local population, provoking hilarious comments in even the Italian Press.[60] More potentially embarrassing was the seizure by Austrian customs of wagon-loads of small arms being smuggled across the border from Italy, in breach of the Treaty of Trianon, en route to Hungary. The difficulty was however solved by the Italian government's promising to take the weapons back as soon as they had been repaired 'according to contract'.[61] The French government, concerned above all else to maintain workable relations with Italy in face of impending changes in Germany, duly declared the matter closed.[62]

The Austrians were the last people to wish to press the matter. Fighting had been taking place in Vienna for months between the local Fascist nationalists, the Heimwehr, and the Austrian Nazis advocating union with Hitlerite Germany. On 4 March, the day before the last free elections in Germany, in which the Nazis gained 44 per cent of the popular vote, Austrian Chancellor Dollfuss declared that parliamentary government was suspended in Austria. There was by now not an effective parliamentary régime left in Europe east of the Rhine. The Fascist Grand Council approvingly noticed an 'affirmation of a new spirit in the Fascist Movement beyond the frontiers of Italy'.[63] The question of course was to what extent Italy could hope to control these new manifestations.

Italian prestige and influence continued to soar. The Four-Power Pact, whose terms, due mainly to French apprehensions,[64] were not exactly precise, was signed on 6 June by the representatives of Britain, France, Germany and Italy. Effectively, it committed the signatories to 'consult together as regards all questions which appertain to them', and to seek 'effective co-operation among all Powers with a view to the maintenance of peace'.[65] Its main significance was however to demonstrate the apparently pacific intentions of the new régime in Germany. Hitler's second-in-command, Goering, had flown to Rome on 20 May to discuss the progress and implications of the Pact with Mussolini, and on 17 June Gombos visited Berlin for the same reason. But hopes of co-operation among the Fascist and quasi-Fascist states were shattered again by developments in Austria. Further rioting between the Nazis and the Heimwehr led Dollfuss to proscribe the Austrian Nazi party on 19 June. Gombos flew to Rome again on 25 July, to investigate rumours that Mussolini was favouring a union of Austria and Hungary under Italian patronage.

Mussolini was at least able to assure Gombos that he was totally opposed to allowing Austria to be absorbed by Germany. He repeated this assurance to Chancellor Dollfuss, who followed Gombos to Rome on 19 August, arriving when the capital was still celebrating the two latest triumphs of Italian technology. The new liner *Rex* had won the Blue Riband of the Atlantic with a speed of 28·92 knots; Marshall Italo Balbo had led a massive armada of eight squadrons of Capronis to Chicago and back; and Captain Agello had secured the world airspeed record for Italy for the next six years, flying a Macchi-Castoldi seaplane at 423 miles per hour.

Dollfuss returned to Vienna, his confidence restored, and announced on 11 September that parliamentary institutions had gone for good in Austria, and 'would never be restored';[66] Premier Duca of Romania was murdered in Bucharest on 28 September by the Italian-inspired, Italian-armed and Italian-financed neophiliacs of the Iron Guard, for daring to suggest that the Guard was inspired, armed and financed by Italy; 100 German airmen were invited secretly to Italy to be trained in bombing techniques by Balbo's swaggering experts; and as 5,000 Blackshirts paraded damply through Manchester of all places, Mussolini spoke proudly to the Grand Council of the triumphant 'march of Fascism through Europe and the world'.[67]

Just as it seemed that all roads were leading to Rome, once again Yugoslavia proved the graveyard of Italian hopes: three Italian-trained Croat Fascists bungled an attempt to assassinate the royal dictator Alexander, on 17 December. But events in

Yugoslavia no longer had any effect on the world outside. On 17 February the Italians obtained from the British and French governments an agreement that they took 'a common view of the necessity of maintaining Austria's independence and integrity in accordance with the relevant treaties', referring specifically to the dossier which the Austrian government had 'prepared with a view to establishing German interference in the internal affairs of Austria . . .'.[68] This was followed on 15 March by the Rome Protocols, affirming the 'independence and rights', of Italy, Austria and Hungary and assuring Hungary of Italian support in the event of an attack by Yugoslavia or any other member of the Little Entente.[69] France then hastened to give its approval to Italian domination in central and eastern Europe, by entering into trade talks with Italy, and on 14 June Hitler came in person to meet the Overlord of the Mediterranean at the Villa Pisani, near Padua.

The initiative had come from the Germans,[70] Hitler apparently having hoped that a face-to-face encounter might help him to gain some personal domination over Mussolini. His chances of doing so, however, were destroyed by Mussolini's great sartorial and linguistic advantages: while Hitler had been persuaded to make himself miserable and uncomfortable in morning clothes the Italian dictator arrived flamboyantly uniformed, and while Hitler spoke no language save his own, Mussolini was thoroughly competent in German, as well as French and English.[71] Nothing definite was agreed upon, or even discussed. Mussolini's impressions of the Nazis remained as mixed as Hitler's impressions of the Fascist leadership. The Italians were confirmed in their contempt for German crudity, and their apprehensions about resurgent German power; the Nazis found it congenial to despise Mussolini for his unrevolutionary traditionalism, but could not help being impressed by the enthusiasm which the Venetian crowds showed for their Duce, however much this might have been inspired by a desire to humiliate their German visitors.[72]

Mussolini had scored a personal success, but his capacity to deter the new revolutionaries north of the Brenner was less than he had imagined. Hitler also was having difficulty: although he had called a halt to Nazi terrorism in Austria while the talks were in progress, Nazi assassination squads murdered Dollfuss on 25 July. Mussolini reacted with fury. Detachments of Alpini were rushed to the Brenner, with air support; and Mussolini denounced Hitler to the leader of the Heimwehr, Starhemberg, as 'a horrible sexual degenerate', and 'a dangerous fool'.[73] The military demonstration had of course been purely for show: there were no German soldiers available to come through Austria to the Brenner, and no reinforcements to support the Alpini ostensibly despatched to confront them. This, however, had not diminished its capacity to encourage the Austrian regime and to discourage its opponents in Austria, something which really annoyed Mussolini. He made his attitude clear when he again ridiculed German intellectual pretensions at Bari on 6 September:

> 'Thirty centuries of history allow us to regard with supreme indulgence certain doctrines taught beyond the Alps by the descendants of people who were wholly illiterate in the days when Caesar, Virgil and Augustus flourished in Rome.'[74]

That the objection was to Nazi assassinations in Austria, not to assassinations as such, was shown however in a matter of weeks. Italian-trained, Italian-sheltered, Italian-armed Croat assassins at last eliminated King Alexander of Yugoslavia on 7 October in Marseilles. The murderers took refuge in their base in Italy. However, new French Foreign Minister Pierre Laval had no intention of forcing Mussolini into an embarrassing position, while Mussolini for his part was determined to reach an accord with France. A workable compromise resulted: claiming to have disarmed members of the Croat terrorist organization, the Ustaci, remaining on Italian territory, the Italians arrested their leader, Ante Pavelic; but instead of extraditing him to stand trial, they merely sent him to hospital. The Yugoslavs, furiously responding by severing commercial relations with Italy, now had no one to whom they could turn for support. Negotiations between Italy and France on security and colonial matters had reached their most serious stage already. Both Great Powers had reason for haste. French Foreign Minister Pierre Laval wanted Italy tied into the French defence system against Germany before the Saar plebiscite was due to be held in the first quarter of 1936.[75] And Mussolini wanted to be sure of French goodwill before embarking on a final solution of African matters then calling for attention.

The most important of these African matters concerned Italy's relations with Abyssinia. Mussolini had been working intermittently since 1929 to secure the Italian predominance in western Abyssinia agreed on by the British in 1925. In 1930 a garrison post was built to confirm Italian control of the watering spot of Walwal, about a hundred miles within the ill-defined south-eastern border of Abyssinia. A major clash occurred there on 5 December 1934 between the Italian garrison and an Abyssinian force sent to eject them. A hundred and seven Abyssinians were killed and forty-five wounded, while the Italian colonial defenders lost about thirty dead and 100 wounded.[76]

A passage of arms around an Abyssinian waterhole had determined the fate of Europe. Emperor Haile Selassie appealed to the League of Nations for arbitration on 14 December 1934. On 20 December Mussolini issued a Directive to his advisers for war against Abyssinia. Laval left for Rome for the final crucial negotiations on a Franco-Italian accord two weeks later, to reach agreement with Mussolini on 7 January. France ceded to Italy 44,000 square miles of central African desert, containing perhaps 900 inhabitants, and 309 square miles of Somali rock, containing probably nobody; the problem of the Italian community in Tunisia was shelved temporarily by allowing children born of Italian parents before 1945 to retain their Italian nationality;* and most importantly, the two partners agreed that no country was entitled to modify its armaments obligations by unilateral action, and that they would act in concert in the event of this happening.[77]

* Those born between 1945 and 1965 were at liberty to adopt French nationality if they chose. After 1965 they would be subject to French legislation

These concessions hardly added up to a monumental diplomatic triumph for the Italians, although they were unquestionably gratifying. Far more important, however, were the military talks that took place between the General Staffs of the two countries, even while the Walwal affair was actually being discussed by the League.[78] France's General Gamelin was 'happy to entertain a proposal from the Italians that their two armies co-operate in case of German aggression against Austria. The French supreme military committee also approved General Gamelin's plan of placing a French army corps between the Italian and the Yugoslav troops in case of war, to act primarily as a bridge between the two unfriendly forces during the drive into Austria where they would link up with the Czechs'.[79] The only real problem appeared to be the British, whose primary interest was that tribes from British Somaliland could cross the area dominated by the Walwal oases, and who had accordingly been negotiating with the Abyssinians for a rectification of the northern frontier of Abyssinia to the advantage of British Somaliland. But the Abyssinians would not be in a position to make the desired rectification unless their own sovereignty over Walwal were effectively recognized.

It could only be expected that the British would resent any expansion of Italian power in east Africa at the expense of Abyssinia, simply because this would make it impossible for the British to do the same. What was completely uncertain was how much importance the British attributed to their imperial frontiers in Somaliland. It was at least possible that they would rate the security and stability of Western Europe as being more important. The Italian Embassy in London sounded Foreign Office opinion on 29 January. Not surprisingly, they were unable to extract anything like a definite statement of British policy.[80]

This very vagueness seemed tantamount to a green light under the circumstances: on 5 February the first Italian divisions left for east Africa via the Suez Canal. Then events took a dramatic new turn which appeared to make Anglo-French-Italian co-operation the more vital to all three Powers. On 15 March the

French government introduced measures to maintain the strength of the French armed forces over the years expected to be affected by the declining birth-rate,[81] and on the following day Hitler introduced conscription in Germany. Negotiations between London, Paris and Rome began immediately; Laval was authorized to leave for Moscow on 20 March; British ministers consulted with the French and Italians in Paris, then left for further talks in Warsaw, Moscow and Prague. Meanwhile, it was announced that British, French and Italian foreign ministers should meet at Stresa on 11 April. A Grand European Design appeared at least to be in the making. It lay under the shadow of Africa.

Mussolini for one left the meeting under the impression that the shadow had been lifted, especially as the representatives of the three Powers agreed on 14 April to sign a Resolution affirming that they found 'themselves in complete agreement in opposing, by all practicable means, any unilateral repudiation of treaties which may endanger the peace, and will act in close and cordial collaboration for this purpose'.[82] Mussolini raised his fountain pen and asked Flandin, Laval, MacDonald and Simon if it was agreed that he should insert after 'peace' the phrase 'in Europe'. He asked again, waiting for the British to respond to this clear intimation of Italian resolve not to keep the peace in Africa. Flandin nodded; Laval smiled; and the British said nothing. The Agreement was signed; and the fate of Abyssinia had been decided.

So had that of the world. It was obvious that the British were not anxious to become involved in a confrontation between the League of Nations and an aggressor, Simon having protested at Geneva on the day following the signature of the Stresa Agreement that 'the whole question of economic reprisals [against an aggressor] was far more complicated than the French seemed to think'.[83] But what was really more complicated for the British than the questions of sanctions was the state of their domestic politics. With unemployment still numbering about 2 million, the Labour Party had in consequence been making substantial gains in by-elections all through 1934. And in November a poll of more than half the total British electorate had recorded a popular vote of sixteen to one in favour of applying economic sanctions against an aggressor, and three to one in favour of military sanctions. The omens were clear: a new political trial of strength in Britain was imminent, and no party could hope to win it which preferred to make a gesture in favour of Stresa, about which the electorate had no feelings, rather than the League of Nations, about which it so clearly had.

The obvious beneficiary of collapse of the Stresa front would be Hitler. Never one to ignore the gifts of Providence, however, Hitler attempted to reassure the Italians by denying any intention of annexing Austria by any means, and regretting that the tension of Austria had disturbed Germany's 'good relations with Italy, a State with whom we otherwise have no conflict of interests'.[84] Meanwhile, the French anxiously attempted to build a solid military structure on the Stresa accords. Units of the French navy visited Venice on 3 June. But on 18 June the British appeared to disregard any notion of Western solidarity entirely, by unilaterally concluding a naval agreement with Germany, under which the Germans would be entitled to construct a fleet with 35 per cent the tonnage of the Royal Navy. This merely irritated the Italians, but it alarmed the French. Laval explained urgently that the League of Nations had now become the basis of France's security system, since it was only in the League that France had a real Entente with the United Kingdom.[85] Meanwhile the British naval build-up in the Mediterranean continued, as it had before in 1923. 144 ships, with a total displacement of 800,000 tons, had assembled by 19 September to safeguard the British imperial life-line through Suez.[86] Winston Churchill claimed rhetorically that for Italy to undertake a war in Abyssinia in such circumstances would be 'to give hostages to fortune unparalleled in all history'.[87] But there is no risk where there is no danger. British politicians agreed with British naval chiefs that a war with Italy in the Mediterranean would leave Britain too weak to defend its empire in the world outside.[88] Italian military advisers similarly could see no way of successfully countering British sea power in the Mediterranean.[89] But they had no need to worry. The United Kingdom was not going to fight a country whose friendship was as important to it as that of Italy. On the other hand, no British Government in the existing state of political delicacy at home was going to ignore a directive such as the gigantic vote of the Trades Union Congress on 5 September, when 2,962,000 unionists against 177,000 affirmed their support for all sanctions against aggression provided by the Covenant of the League of Nations. The Conservatives had their priorities clear. They would allow Abyssinia to be conquered; they would allow the unity of western Europe to be shattered; and they would win the next election.

Italian forces invaded Abyssinia without a declaration of war on 2 October 1935; Britain and France, along with all other members of the League except Austria and Hungary, applied economic sanctions against Italy; and a desperate attempt by Hoare and Pierre Laval to escape the issue by arranging a partition of Abyssinia was dropped in the face of British public opinion and Mussolini's demand for political control of Abyssinia. Sanctions were maintained, but without being extended to the vital war requirements of coal, steel or oil. They did, however, cut Italy's foreign trade and reserves of foreign exchange by more than a half; British exports to Italy had fallen from £6 million to £225,000 by the first quarter of 1936. The effect of this mitigated economic pressure was to mass the Italian people behind Mussolini; to impose some very real constraints upon the Italian war effort in 1935; and to inspire Mussolini to demand substantially greater efforts in 1936.

These were made all the easier by the sudden collapse of the British commitment to sanctions in March 1936. The Italians had begun seriously experimenting with new forms of MAS-boats in January, as a means of countering British naval supremacy in the Mediterranean. All concern about what the British might still do was, however, removed by Hitler's occupation of the Rhineland on 7 March. France and Britain began talks with the Italians at once, on a basis of an undertaking not to extend sanctions. As a result, the Italians decided they could now risk an unrestrained offensive. Fascist Secretary-General Starace led an armoured column in a whirlwind charge to Lake Tana, covering 340 miles in fourteen days, admittedly unimpeded by any effective opposition,[90] and on 27 March Mussolini boasted that the Italian air force controlled the Mediterranean, annulling British naval supremacy. It was even rumoured that the Duce had called for seventy volunteers to fly on suicide raids against the British fleet, and that 700 airmen had answered this unusual demand on their services.[91] On 5 May Badoglio's vanguard entered Addis Ababa. It was enough of a lesson for the Balkans: the Yugoslavs and their neighbours decided in Belgrade on 15 May that they should be free to adopt whatever attitude they chose towards Germany and Italy, without regard for the provisions of the League Covenant. Yugoslav Foreign Minister Purić also reproved Britain's Anthony Eden sharply for not seeming to know what he wanted, and warned him that Britain would have to be prepared to fight for its empire in the Mediterranean, or lose it.[92]

There was at least one thing that the British did want to do: they wanted at last to try to mend relations with Italy, now that Abyssinia no longer existed to complicate them. When Chamberlain spoke in favour of abandoning sanctions on 10 June, the Italian triumph was apparently complete. Mussolini had defied the League and had successfully fought the biggest colonial war in history. He had mobilized 476,542 men, with 1,542 guns, 938 tanks and 400 aircraft against a total Abyssinian deployment of 350,000 men with 200 guns; he had lost 1,537 soldiers killed in action against an estimated 28,000 Abyssinian dead; and he had fought the first thoroughly modern war of the century.[93] His aviation provided the model for the Blitzkriegs of the future, supporting, guiding and supplying the Italian armoured columns. He had, however, also expended 17,000 million lire at a time when Italian industrial output had sunk to its lowest level since 1933.[94] It was therefore time for a rest. But this was precisely what Mussolini chose to deny his country. On the night of 16–17 July a military rising against the domestic Republican government had begun in Melilla, in Spanish Morocco, and on 19 July Francisco Franco formally asked the Italian government for aircraft and bombs.[95] There were many factors inducing Mussolini to respond sympathetically to such a request. Most important was undoubtedly the belief, shared by almost every national leader who has involved his country in an unnecessary war, that the involvement would be brief and inexpensive. Next was simple euphoria: Italy had impressively won an incontestable and total victory in Abyssinia, and Italy was a country which could always use another total victory to enhance its credibility as a Great Power, especially at a time when that credibility was being challenged by German resurgence. There were also possible material advantages to be gained from helping Franco and the Falange to come to power in Spain: there were the prospects of assured access to Spanish raw materials; of the use of Spanish naval bases in the Balearics; of pressure being placed on both the British and French by an Italian-aligned quasi-Fascist Spain; of the strategic and diplomatic benefits to be gained by extending Italian predominance to the western Mediterranean as it had already been extended to south-eastern Europe. Finally, there was strong attraction in the idea of repairing Fascist relations with the Vatican by assisting a cause in Spain which had been endorsed by the Pope.

On 25 July Mussolini agreed to provide aircraft.[96] Hitler also agreed to a similar request the following day. France had already sent equipment to the Spanish government. The inevitable effect of all this was to deepen the rift between Italy and the West. When on 7 September the British, concerned at any alteration in the strategic and diplomatic position in the western Mediterranean, criticized the Italians for their intervention, their charges were dismissed frivolously by Galeazzo Ciano, Mussolini's son-in-law and Minister of Foreign Affairs. Hitler took quite the opposite point of view. On 24 October he climaxed his cordial references to Mussolini by formally recognizing the annexation of Abyssinia to the Italian empire, in gratitude for which, Mussolini in a speech eight days later remarked that the accord between Germany and Italy was coming to represent 'a kind of axis'.[97]

The result of all this was that Italy now had no option but to come to some kind of accord with the new Germany, at least until some effective relationship could be revived with Britain and France. And Italian predominance in south-eastern Europe was already being challenged by German economic power. In the period 1926–30 Yugoslavia had transacted 19 per cent of its total foreign trade with Italy, and only 12·3 per cent with Germany; in 1931–35 the respective figures were 17 and 15 per cent; and in 1936–39, 7·6 and 31·5 per cent.[98] The Hungarian Regent Horthy, having sacked Gombos, anxiously conferred with Ciano in Rome on 12 November about the decline in Italian purchases of Hungarian wheat.[99] The strain of another war was beginning to tell.

For the fact was that Italian Fascism, unlike German National Socialism, never seemed able to insulate the Italian economy to any notable degree from the vicissitudes of depression and recovery in the world outside. Nazi Germany escaped almost entirely the effects of the startlingly severe recessions of mid-1937 and mid-1938, and responded only marginally to those of December 1938 and January 1939, whereas Italy responded more drastically to swings in the international trade cycle than any other major European Power.

Italy nevertheless continued positively to enhance its diplomatic prestige. On 2 January 1937 an agreement was reached with Britain, affirming the independence of Spain and freedom of passage through the Mediterranean. The Yugoslavs, immediately concluding that the West could not be relied upon to afford protection against Italy, which it was obviously seeking to placate, rejected a French offer of a mutual assistance pact and began negotiations directly with Rome.[100] But Italy's bargaining position, fortified by the impressive showing of its aviation at Malaga in January, was jeopardized by a shambles at Guadalajara on 11 March, where the Italian forces, mainly ill-trained, irregular rowdies of the Fascist Youth, suffered more casualties than they had in the whole Abyssinian campaign. There was now no alternative to all-out victory in Spain – 60,000 Italian troops, with 1,930 guns, 950 tanks and 763 aircraft were rushed there.[101] In material terms, it was a bigger effort than the Abyssinian campaign; it cost nearly half as much; it put a stop to urgently needed retraining and re-equipment of the Italian armed forces; and it precipitated a further recession of the Italian economy.[102] But Mussolini was winning the victories he wanted: a pact 'of peace and security' was reached with Premier Stojadinovic of Yugoslavia on 25 March; on 31 July, the Japanese, impressed by Mussolini's defiant boast of intervention in Spain, began cautious approaches for an anti-Comintern Accord; on 7 August Italian aircraft and submarines began indiscriminate attacks on merchant ships which might be carrying Russian arms to the Spanish government; and on 18 August Italian armoured columns broke through the Republican front before Santander.[103] Meanwhile the highly unofficial Italian naval and air blockade was intensified with what can only be described as amazing disregard for international delicacies.

> 'On 26 August a British ship was bombed off Barcelona. On 29 August a Spanish steamer was shelled by a submarine off the French coast. A French passenger steamer reported that she was chased by a submarine into the Dardanelles. On the 30th the Russian merchantman *Tuniyaev* was sunk at Algiers. . . . On 31 August a submarine attacked the British destroyer *Havock*. . . . On 1 September the Russian steamer *Blagaev* was sunk by a submarine off Skyros. On 2 September the British tanker *Woodford* was sunk near Valencia. "Three torpedoings and one prize", Ciano remarked in his diary on that day. . . .'[104]

This wild hunt was halted by a decision at Nyon that the Mediterranean west of Malta should be patrolled by the British and French navies, which should attack any suspicious submarine. However, a subsequent agreement of 27 September allotted the Italians a patrol zone, presumably to keep an eye on themselves, between the Balearic Islands and Sardinia, as well as in the Tyrrhenian Sea. They were thus able to continue sending supplies to Franco at Majorca without being observed.

This was highly impressive and in many ways satisfactory, but again the person to whom it was most satisfactory was Hitler. Every Italian diplomat or military coup had the unintended effect of strengthening ties with Germany. On 6 November, Ciano signed a protocol providing for the adherence of Italy to the Anti-Comintern Pact, already entered into by Germany and Japan against the alleged efforts of International Communism 'continuously to endanger the civilized world in the East and the West'. On the day before, Hitler had informed his commanders-in-chief that 'it must be our first aim in every case of entanglement by war to conquer Czechoslovakia and Austria simultaneously . . .'.

For Italy and Europe were now caught up without their knowledge in the Nazi timetable. Any substantial readjustment of Germany's frontiers could be carried out with reasonable safety only before British and Russian rearmament had made the odds against Germany quite impossible. On 11 March 1938 Hitler reminded Mussolini of how he had showed sympathy for the Italians in their 'critical hour' in the Abyssinian crisis, also promising that if Mussolini 'should ever be in any great need or danger, he could be certain that I will protect him to the uttermost, whatever may happen, even if the world should rise against him . . .'.[105] Austria was absorbed into the Reich on the following day. Hitler reiterated his promises never to forget Mussolini on the 13th. Mussolini for his part explained to the Italian people on 16 March that he had never assumed any obligation to defend the independence of Austria, and that the Rome-Berlin Axis had 'proved itself particularly solid at this critical point of the history of the German world of Europe'.[106]

More importantly, the Italians intervened to prevent any ill-treatment of deposed Austrian Chancellor Scuschnigg by the Germans. Hitler, being particularly concerned to placate the Italians in any possible way, because of their fear that Italian bellicosity might well start a war somewhere in Europe, was fully prepared to oblige: the Nazi timetable required that Mussolini should be calmed down. This was actually achieved by a completely one-sided Agreement between Italy and the United Kingdom on 16 April, under which the Italians undertook to preserve the *status quo* in the Mediterranean and to withdraw their forces from Spain, once the Civil War was over.[107] This was scarcely a *rapprochement* between Italy and the West, but it was at least a *detente*. It had no time to develop, however, for the Nazi timetable took charge again. Nazi leaders in Bohemia, acting on Hitler's orders, demanded on 24 April that the Czechoslovakian government approve the full autonomy of the German Sudetenland in Bohemia as a Nazi state. As staff talks began between the British and French, Hitler hastily set off on a state visit to Italy. The two leaders promised eternal friendship to each other, but Mussolini persistently became non-committal when Hitler spoke of a binding alliance, as he did on at least three occasions.[108] Involvement with Spain meant that Italy was in no condition to accept any further military commitments. In any case, when Galeazzo Ciano visited Tirana on 2 May for King Zog's wedding to a Hungarian princess, he had been concerned by rumours of German interest in the Adriatic.

Without the Italian alliance, Hitler could not face the combination of Britain, France, Russia and Czechoslovakia which it appeared he was faced with. Negotiations were reopened on 23 May between the Czech government and the Sudeten leaders, and on 28 May Hitler ordered his commanders-in-chief to be prepared to 'smash Czechoslovakia' on 1 October 1938. Meanwhile, the Yugoslavs, playing their new double game of balancing between Rome and Berlin, continued to harass Ciano with warnings of German Balkan ambitions. The new Czech crisis exploded on 12 September, when a ferocious speech by Hitler at a Nuremberg rally signalled the start of an abortive rebellion by the Sudeten Germans. On 15 September Mussolini called for a plebiscite in the disputed area while British Prime Minister Neville Chamberlain flew to see Hitler at Berchtesgaden, to seek a peaceful division of Czechoslovakia. But a German demand that the Czechs evacuate the Sudetenland by 1 October was rejected by London, Paris and Prague on 24 September. For four days, Europe waited for war. On 28 September Mussolini desperately appealed to a seriously concerned Hitler to delay mobilization and resume negotiations with the British.

It was the last triumph of Conference Europe. Once again Mussolini saw his concept of the Four-Power Directorate revived, as he presided over a meeting of British, French, German and Italian representatives, from which the Czechs and Russians were pointedly excluded, to arrange the partitioning of Czechoslovakia. The Italian contribution was by no means irresponsible: on one occasion Mussolini argued for a plebiscite in Bohemia, but was overruled by the British and French, who had no wish to see a peaceful settlement jeopardized by allowing the people concerned a choice in determining which government they would prefer to live under.

The success of the Munich Conference inspired Hitler to propose a military alliance to Mussolini again, on 30 September. But the Italian leader had new worries: while the Munich Conference had reaffirmed Italy's role as the true balance of power in Europe, it had also enormously strengthened the power of Germany. It had also shown that the British and French could simply not be trusted to impose any real constraints on future German expansion. There accordingly seemed little else for Italy to do except enter into a formal alliance with Nazi Germany, if only as a means of exercising some control over the direction of Nazi policy, since the West seemed unwilling to accept this task by any other means.

But there was still some unfinished business to be dealt with first: German movement in the Balkans had to be forestalled by the establishment of an Italian military presence there. Military adventure of any sort would of course be overstraining Italy's resources, but the risk had to be taken. In a reversal of usual military priorities, which revealed all too clearly the problems of Italy's war economy, Mussolini sold combat aircraft to the

7a. Mussolini sighting a mortar gun at military manoeuvres

7b. Mussolini receiving gifts on his arrival to open an exhibition of work done by Italian workmen's clubs

8. 2 December 1943: Italian surrender to Nazi storm-troopers in Rome

French government in October, in exchange for raw materials. King Zog, observing the military preparations on the other side of the Adriatic, appealed pitifully to the Italians not to invade his country, on the grounds that they owned it already.[109]

Mussolini was in fact still undecided. He replied evasively to yet another offer of an alliance by Ribbentrop on 28 October, on the day that 20,000 Italians set sail for Africa, in the greatest single migration fleet in history, to join the 160,000 who had already gone there over the past three years.[110] There was still one inducement, however, which could have been offered to Italy to abandon the Balkans in return for gratification elsewhere. On 30 November Mussolini talked of 'the natural aspirations of the Italian people', meaning specifically their hankerings after Nice, Tunis and Savoy, and possibly Corsica. The offer of a single French department or imperial province might even at this stage have been sufficient to attract Italy away from the German alliance, and thus make German aggression militarily impossible. But Paris was no more capable in 1938 than Vienna had been in 1914 of sacrificing a province to save an empire. The French might be too scared to fight the Germans alone, but they were not scared enough to pay the price necessary to ensure that they would never have to. Foreign Minister Francois-Poncet boasted on 1 December that the Italians would have to learn that the road to Tunis ran over the bodies of 45 million Frenchmen.[111] The road to Paris did not run over so many in 1940.

Mussolini turned back to the Balkans. On 19 December Ciano went to Budapest as the guest of Regent Horthy, to discuss Hungary's adherence to the Axis, and to assure Hungary of Italian support if Hungary were attacked by 'the universally hated German Reich'. Meanwhile in Spain, Italian armour won the last great battle of the Civil War, smashing through the Republican defences on the Ebro and sweeping on to Barcelona.[112] Mussolini made his mind up at last, on hearing that a Franco-British military compact had at last been arrived at. Ciano was told to write to Ribbentrop accepting the proposal to transform the Anti-Comintern Pact into a Triple Alliance.

Ribbentrop responded immediately, but negotiations were held up again while Ciano went to Belgrade on 18 January, to assure himself that the new government there would not oppose an Italian occupation of Albania.

The Yugoslavs were of course fully prepared to condone any move by Italy which seemed likely to worsen that country's relations with Germany. But once again it was Germany which dictated the tempo of events. On 6 March 1939 Hitler threatened Czechoslovakia with war again, after the breakdown of negotiations between the Prague government and nationalist movements in Ruthenia and Slovakia, and on 15 March Czechoslovakia ceased to exist as a nation. Panic swept through the Balkans again. On 16 March Mussolini sent a warning to Berlin to leave Croatia alone. Hitler immediately responded docilely, recognizing the Mediterraneans as a basically Italian sphere of interest. Mussolini, who had decided in the interim to drop the idea of a German alliance, now swung back on 21 March to a policy 'of unalterable fidelity to the Axis'. There seemed little point at this stage in anything but siding with the winner. The Albanian affair was therefore quickly disposed of. An untimatum was sent to Zog on 25 March; Ciano arranged with Horthy for a partial Hungarian mobilization on the Yugoslav frontier, to discourage any last-minute thoughts of intervention in Belgrade;[113] and Albania was overrun in a simple amphibious operation on 7 April. The Italian system in the Balkans was still effective.

It was, however, a system that depended on the maintenance of peace in Europe for at least another six years. Italy needed time for everything: to pacify the empire, to complete its programme of naval construction, to accumulate reserves of fuel and raw materials, to disperse its industry out of the range of French and British bombers, to re-equip completely its army and air force, and above all to develop new types of fighter aircraft comparable with the latest models being developed by the British and Germans. It was thus with real urgency that Mussolini assured the world on 14 May that the existing circumstances in Europe would not justify war.[114]

But war was exactly what Hitler had planned. Whereas Mussolini saw the Alliance as a brake on Germany, Hitler saw it as a green light. The Italian interpretation was justified by the actual wording of the Pact of Steel, signed in Berlin on 22 May. It admittedly involved a total commitment on either party to come to the other's aid in the event of war, however entered upon. But Article II of the Pact also bound the High Contracting Parties to consult with each other immediately 'should their common interests be endangered through international events'. Article II was the only reason why the Italians signed the Pact of Steel, and it was the only article in it that meant nothing to the Germans. On the day after the Pact was signed, without any word to the Italians, Hitler ordered the planning of Operation White against Poland, on 1 September.

Meanwhile, the Italians were coming home from Spain. The airmen, the tank crews, the artillerymen who had won the war for Franco returned to a heroes' welcome, after three years of fighting, in which they had lost 6,000 dead, nearly four times as many as had been killed in the Abyssinian campaign.[115] But there was still no pause for reconstruction. On 19 July Mussolini was still talking about 'a period of well-being and tranquility'. He suggested that the troubles between Germany and Poland could be solved through the traditional Italian technique of a European conference, but this idea was dismissed by Ribbentrop on 25 July. Then on 12 August Hitler made clear his intention to go to war with Poland, though without necessarily seeking Italian help in a 'localized war'. Mussolini continued to plead for some gesture of peaceful intent. A slightly more successful bid was made on 26 August, after the British-Polish Treaty had been signed, and three days after the completion of the Russo-German Non-Aggression Pact, with which Hitler hoped 'to tie the hands of the West'. Ciano conveyed to Ribbentrop Italy's requirements from Germany in order to be able to fight a major war for twelve months. They amounted to 7 million tons of oil, 6 million tons of coal, 2 million tons of steel, and one million tons of timber, besides small quantities of rubber, copper and the rarer metals. In order to protect Italy's industrial quadrilateral, Turin-Genoa-Milan-Savona . . . a hundred and fifty A.A. batteries with ammunition were necessary'.[116]

Ciano remarked with satisfaction that the list would have choked a bull, if the bull could have read it. It was not, however, excessive, for Italy needed everything. The navy had in reserve enough petrol for one year's action.[117] Fascist wings flew higher as well as faster than anybody else's, since Mario Pezzi had soared to 56,017 feet, to add the world's altitude record to Agello's air-speed triumph; but the Regia Aeronautica was being supplied by Italian industry only with 'little bombs, suitable for civil or colonial wars'.[118] The whole Italian aircraft industry was plagued 'by protection, by monopolies, by shortage of capital',[119] as well as by corruption. Its failings were endless. An excellent aerial torpedo had been developed in Fiume in 1937, but had been rejected by the Regia Aeronautica after a disagreement with the navy over who was to pay; then 300 torpedoes were sold to the Germans and Italy was left without a torpedo-bomber squadron, despite the fact that it had been the first country to develop this weapon.[120] Similarly, the Italian aircraft industry 'could develop a 3,300 horsepower engine with which to win the world's air-speed record, but not a 1,000–1,500 horsepower engine for its fighters'.[121] The country which had invented wireless transmission had not provided efficient sets for its aircraft; it had built the best tank in the world in 1918, but now it possessed barely 100 inferior medium tanks in 1939. To complete the picture, the army was still relying on the same model rifle with which it had first been issued in 1891.[122]

Hitler bit on the bullet. He explained that although he understood Mussolini's position, German plans could not be halted this time by Italian proposals for a conference. And Mussolini had other problems as well. Fascist but hostile Greece mobilized partially on 24 August,[123] in response to which he was forced to call 1,800,000 men to the colours. Meanwhile he continued to press for a European conference, even after the German attack on Poland had commenced on 1 September. For the next two days the British and the French were still prepared to investigate the prospects of a conference solution, but only if the German forces in Poland were to withdraw to the original frontier.[124] The Italian intervention had failed, and one of the greatest tragedies in human history had begun.

The outbreak of war produced no real change in Italian policies. Mussolini and Ciano reiterated their desire for peace at every opportunity, alarmed as they were by their knowledge of Italy's military unreadiness, by the impact on the Italian economy of the British and French naval blockade, and by their concern over possible Russian expansion in the Balkans, under the blessing of the Russo-German Pact. Dislike of Russia was magnified by Stalin's attack on Finland on 1 December. Italy joined with the West in rushing military aid to the Finns, until appealed to urgently by Hitler to desist, on the grounds that he, Hitler, would be contravening the Russo-German Pact if he continued to allow Italian aid to be sent to Finland across German territory. Tensions between the two Axis Powers reached a new peak on 16 December when Ciano, in a two-hour oration, deplored the Russo-German Pact, the German decision to go to war in 1939 after assuring Italy that Europe needed at least another three years' peace, and the German failures to respond to Italy's appeals for a conference. Mussolini wrote to Hitler on 1 January 1940, suggesting that it might 'cost too much' to try to bring the Allies to their knees by military action.

But the reality was unchanged: while the Allies could not or would not offer Italy anything, Hitler could promise territorial expansion and military glory, and was prepared to give in the meantime flattery and coal. After the two dictators met again in Rome on 10 March, massive trainloads of coal began to move south from Germany to Italy's industrial centres, still starved by the Allied blockade.[125] Italy could scarcely have withheld support from the country which provided the means for its economic existence. But more urgent reasons for entering the war became apparent after 10 May 1940. By the end of that month French defeat appeared to be only a matter of time. There could be no rational expectation that the British would be able to continue hostilities successfully after 25 May. Nor could Italy expect to retain anything like an influential role in a Europe dominated by the Germans and Russians unless it made at least a gesture towards military participation. The fact that the Italians were in no shape to fight and from the German point of view had no need to fight did not of course make any difference. On 29 May Mussolini told his chiefs of staff that he intended to intervene at any time after 5 June. There was no question this time of victory or defeat – the issue was the preservation of a Balance of Power in Europe.

5 : To Lose an Empire

ITALY would have been justified in going to war only if it could have been certain that it would not have to fight, which was not an unreasonable expectation, as British military advisers had already recorded their opinion that Germany held most of the cards.[1] There was of course no question of Hitler's desiring to reach a peaceful accommodation with the British, but then it seemed probable that the Germans would be able to impose a military solution on a government in London if they were forced to do so. What was equally evident, however, was that the Italian Empire would be in a militarily hopeless position if the British were able to fend off a German attack on the home islands. The Italian fleet in the Mediterranean was outnumbered seriously by the British and French in almost every category of fighting ship. The Italians could deploy on 30 May four battleships actually ready for action against two French and four British battleships and a battle cruiser; seven 8-inch gun cruisers against seven French ships of the same class; twelve 6-inch gun cruisers against seven French and nine British; and fifty fleet destroyers against thirty-five French and thirty-two British.[2] They certainly had the most numerous submarine service in the world, with 115 undersea craft against a combined Anglo-French force of fifty. But five of these 115 were prototypes, abandoned when hostilities broke out; only forty-two were suitable for ocean-going service; and even these carried no more than half the torpedo complement of the German U-boats, were three knots on average slower, and took more than twice as long to submerge.[3] Perhaps most important was the lack of an aircraft-carrier of any kind, while the British had at Alexandria the ancient *Eagle,* with seventeen Swordfish torpedo-bombers and three Gladiator biplane fighters, which could certainly present a serious threat to a fleet with neither.[4]

The Italian navy was thus in effect committed to remaining on the defensive within the protection of its land-based air cover, at least until the French had been eliminated. But this in turn meant abandoning the Italian Empire in North Africa to attack by substantially stronger Anglo-French forces. Total Italian forces in Libya amounted on 30 May to 167,000 men, seriously demoralized by the experience of military service in the desert, with 1,600 guns, 339 tanks, 315 aircraft of which barely 151 were effective, and forty-four anti-tank guns, useless against two-thirds of British armour. Against them, the British and French could assemble in North Africa about 419,000 men, with 900 aircraft and 300 tanks.[5] Only in Abyssinia, where the Duke of Aosta commanded about 280,000 men, with 400 guns, 323 aircraft and fifty-three tanks, could the Italian military position be considered reasonably secure.[6]

Logic thus suggested that the war for the control of Africa and the Mediterranean would have to be decided in the fields of France and the skies over Britain, and the Italians were in no shape to make an effective contribution to either. Italian strategy was thus hamstrung from the start, in much the same way as it had been in 1866.[7] The world waited for the torrential sweep of the Italian torpedo striking force, 'the occupation of Malta, the blocking with a mine field of the Suez Canal, an active demonstration by the Fleet, a massive bombardment of Alexandria; and instead we were immobile, strictly on the defensive'.[8] In fact it was the Anglo-French who took the offensive, as their superior strength entitled them to do. Two battleships, an aircraft carrier, eleven cruisers and twelve destroyers swept the Mediterranean from bases at Alexandria, Port Said and Beirut. At the same time, aircraft from Egypt bombed and damaged the Italian cruiser *San Giorgio* in Tobruk. But first blood went to the Italians. The submarine *Bagnolini* sank the British light cruiser *Calypso* on 12 June. This was not, however, what it seemed to be: the first blow in a massive submarine campaign. The major submarine offensive was actually opened by the British from Alexandria and Malta, and by the French from Beirut; on 11 June British units crossed the Libyan border from Egypt, surprising Italian troops who had not yet been informed that they were at war;[9] and on 12 June two French heavy cruisers bombarded Genoa, to be driven off eventually by the coastal batteries and a solitary MAS.[10]

None of this was really very inspiring, but then no offensive action against France could make much sense, as the French were clearly on the point of collapse after June 12 anyway. However a gesture had to be made, and the Regia Aeronautica was despatched on a flurry of raids on Toulon and other towns in southern France. Meanwhile, the available divisions of the Italian army were hastily organized for an attack on the strongest defensive position left in Europe, an assault which could serve no military purpose and gain no glory whatever, against an enemy. And this enemy who could be counted on to fight at its incomparable best, to show that Frenchmen could still beat Italians, even if they were at that moment being beaten all along the line by Germans. The Battle of the Alps proved to be as great a disaster as could have been expected. Twenty Italian divisions, about 312,500 men in all, barely half of them equipped for modern mobile warfare, attacked almost impregnable positions held by six French divisions, 175,000 strong.[11] They had still made virtually no headway when the French surrendered to Germany on 24 June, after losing 186 dead, against Italian losses of 1,200 dead and 1,141 taken prisoner. Nor had the air force performed more impressively. A bag of ten French aircraft destroyed in the air or on the ground did not compensate for a loss of 101 Italian aircraft, by combat, accident or incompetent servicing.[12]

The message was clear: Italy was in no condition to fight a war against a Great Power – Ciano's forecasts had been perfectly correct. It was also clear that the authorities in Rome had no idea what kind of a war they were supposed to fight. The air force, stupefied with the dogmas of Douhet, had been expended in a totally useless and terribly expensive bombardment of the French positions in the Alps;[13] the navy was hamstrung by the strategy of 'the Fleet in Being, the doctrine of the secondary, inferior Fleet, of the French during the naval wars of the 18th century';[14] and Italian numerical superiority at sea was dissipated in ill-considered engagements blundered into by inexperienced sailors, without radar, training in night actions, or adequate air reconnaissance, against a fleet equipped with all of these, and manned by the most confident and ablest sailors on that side of the world. On 26 June the destroyer *Espero* was sunk, after a duel between two Italian destroyers mounting twelve 4·7-inch guns, against five British cruisers, with forty-eight 6-inch guns.[15] Two Italian submarines were destroyed on the following day. Then on 28 June the British moved reinforcements into the Mediterranean, confronting the Italians with a further three capital ships, another light cruiser, four more destroyers and another aircraft carrier, with twenty-four Skua fighter dive-bombers, and thirty Swordfish torpedo-bombers. On the same day, Italy's scant supply of leadership was tragically diminished when Italo Balbo was shot down over Tobruk by his own anti-aircraft gunners, who mistook the Savoia S79 he was flying for a British Blenheim, a number of which had just been attacking Tobruk from the same direction in which Balbo was flying.[16]

Although it was too early yet to say that everything was going wrong, none of this was exactly auspicious. And Italian morale was not raised by a terrifying demonstration of British determination to resist, as well as of British naval power, when the French squadron was attacked in the harbour at Mers-el-Kebir on 3 July. After this, Aosta began to push into the Sudan, capturing the towns of Kassala and Gallabat just across the border on 4 July, to suffer an utterly uneconomic loss of 117 men, in exchange for a mere ten British casualties. Meanwhile, Mussolini ordered his high command to prepare for a full-scale war against

Yugoslavia, for a limited action against Greece, and for a landing in Corsica; at the same time he was also offering Hitler aircraft for use against Britain, and promising Balbo's successor, Graziani, that all necessary tanks and motorized equipment should be sent to Libya.[17]

Italy was fighting on too many fronts already. On 5 July the destroyer *Zeffiro,* already damaged in the inappropriately gallant affair of 29 June, was sunk by Swordfish in Benghasi harbour. One thing at least had to be done: Libya had to be reinforced. Admiral Campioni put to sea with a huge force of two battleships, sixteen cruisers and thirty-two destroyers, to escort five merchant ships with supplies for Graziani. The British Admiral Cunningham was also at sea, with three battleships, five cruisers and sixteen destroyers, and with the old aircraft carrier *Eagle,* to cover the passage of two British convoys from Malta to Alexandria. The resulting action was extraordinary in many ways. Campioni was of course crippled by the dogmatic insistence of Chief of Staff, Badoglio, that the pursuit of a naval battle as an end in itself was ridiculous.[18] He accordingly resolved to avoid a fight to the finish in the open sea, which could only result in his own fleet's suffering heavily, and attempted to draw the British inshore, where they could be destroyed by the bombers of the Regia Aeronautica in comparative safety. The British for their part hoped to avoid anything of the kind, and sought to force the more lightly armed Italian battleships to stop and fight, by slowing them down with airborne torpedo attacks. Nothing worked. The convoys all got through; the British carrier-based torpedo-bombers missed with all their attacks; and the Regia Aeronautica carried out seventy-two attacks on the British fleet, and 124 attacks on their own fleet, with great precision and determination. They did not, however, manage to hit either their own ships or the British, although they escaped being hit by British and Italian anti-aircraft fire.[19] Calabria may not have been exactly 'a battle of the fearful'; but there was not much likelihood of a decision being reached in the Mediterranean, unless either the British or the Italians changed their style of fighting.[20] For the fact was, as Franco's former Chief of Air Staff wisely observed, that neither Britain nor Italy was really adequately prepared for the new style of air-naval war.[21] Both navies suffered from the assumption that they could rely on land-based air support, from independent air services, with the result that the Italians had no naval air service at all, and that the British fleet air arm was tragically weak and equipped with antiquated aircraft, unsuited for combat against a modern land-based air force, because it had been assumed that this role would be carried out by the R.A.F. The Japanese and United States navies on the other hand had proceeded on the assumption that they would be doing their fighting, naturally against each other, far beyond the range of land-based air support, and had accordingly developed vast, self-reliant air arms, fully capable as events proved, of matching in quality and numbers any shore-based opposition they were likely to encounter.

For the time being, ships had to fight ships, but this did not help the Italians. When on 19 July two Italian 6-inch gun cruisers encountered a British cruiser of similar class, the *Sydney,* off Cape Spada, one of the Italians was sunk. Seven weeks of war had cost Italy so far a cruiser, two destroyers and nine submarines, against British losses of a cruiser and five submarines, while casualties in the air and on land were running at a steady level of ten to one, in favour of the British.

It was none the less still very easy to believe that time was running out for the British. The Italians had already reoccupied the last Italian territory conquered by British troops, when they retook Forts Capuzzo and Maddelena in Libya, at a cost in casualties of something like thirty to one; they were probing cautiously into Kenya as well as the Sudan, capturing the frontier post of Moyale; and in any case the Germans decided on their full-scale air offensive against Britain on 2 August, which was expected to bring the war to an end within a month or so. On the following day, Aosta began the invasion of British Somaliland. Faced with the alternatives of either withdrawing their hopelessly outnumbered forces in order to avoid futile losses, or of strengthening them to make resistance practicable, the British decided to do neither. They chose to absorb another military defeat, at a time when the world was wondering if they could ever win a victory.

Italian occupation of Somaliland was completed on 18 August. Once again it involved a most uneconomic exchange of casualties: this time 2,052 against 260. It also coincided with the defeat of the first stage of the German assault on Britain. Victory was not exactly around the corner for the Axis Powers.

This was not the only problem the Axis leaders now had to face. On 16 August Ribbentrop had warned Ciano against attacking Yugoslavia, for fear that it might lead to Russian intervention before the British had been safely dealt with.[22] But Italy's position in the Balkans was seriously called in question between 26 and 29 August, when Ribbentrop imposed an appallingly rough-and-ready solution of the Transylvanian dispute upon Hungary and Romania, compelling the latter to cede two-thirds of the debated territory to Hungary.[23] One immediate consequence was the abdication of King Carol of Romania, and his replacement as Head of State by Antonescu, who gave every apparent indication that he would supinely co-operate with Hitler. There would soon be little of the Balkans left for Italy to assert its authority in. And there was no longer any point in waiting for an early British surrender. Although up till now honours had been fairly even in the second stage of the Battle of Britain, by the third stage it was already evident not only that the attempt to drive the British from the skies of southern England had failed, but that they were present there in numbers greater than ever before. The invasion could never take place at this rate. It was time for Italy to move.

Peremptory orders from Mussolini at last forced Graziani over the Egyptian border on 13 September. It was already too late: sixty Hurricanes and forty-eight Blenheim Mark IV fighters were on the way to Egypt from Britain, to redress the balance of the air war in Egypt, and worse still, a convoy of over 100 tanks was due to reach Egypt by 24 September. Graziani's only hope would have been to make an all-out dash for Alexandria, for which he lacked the equipment, the expertise, and the disposition. The Italians advanced about thirty-five miles to just beyond the airfield of Sidi Barrani, where they stopped on 16 September, and before Graziani could move again, the whole nature of the war had altered.

It all happened very quickly. Hitler called off the invasion of Britain on 17 September, after the decisive defeat of the Luftwaffe two days before. Meanwhile, British torpedo-bombers sank another Italian destroyer in Benghasi harbour, and laid mines which sank yet another. But at last the Italians had an aircraft, a weapon and a body of fliers who could strike back. Although Italy still did not have a single squadron of torpedo-bombers, thanks to disputes between the navy and the Regia Aeronautica as to who should have the honour of commanding such a force, if it were ever formed,[24] it did have what was at the time perhaps the best torpedo-bomber in the world, the Savoia S79, superior in every way to the British Blenheim, and more heavily armed than the German Ju88. It was one of these which put the British cruiser *Kent* permanently out of action on the night of 17 September, thus foreshadowing Italy's last bid for victory at sea two years later.

But even the S79 could not operate effectively without some fighter cover, and events were making it clear that Italy did not yet have an aircraft which could hope to survive in combat with the eight-gun interceptors that the British had developed. Italian aircraft had been sent to Belgium at the end of September, to help replace the losses suffered by the Luftwaffe, despite earlier German objections that the Italian aircraft lacked armour and that their pilots were not trained in flying blind.[25] In two sorties against England they lost six of their own aircraft, without being able to inflict any casualties on the British. Even the lumbering Fulmars, fifteen of which gave the Mediterranean Fleet its nearest approach to modern carrier-based fighter protection, had been able to massacre twenty-one Italian aircraft for a loss of only one of their own number.[26]

All this was not lost on Graziani, trapped as he was in the country east of Sidi Barrani, facing attack by an enemy whose aircraft could shoot his own down at will, whose guns could destroy any Italian tanks, and two-thirds of whose own tanks could not be stopped by any Italian anti-tank gun.[27] To add to his alarm was the discovery that his front was no longer to be regarded as Italy's most important. Mussolini had told Hitler on 19 October that he intended to settle accounts with Greece shortly.[28] The Duce had himself been told by Ribbentrop, who could always be counted on for any indiscretion so long as it was both stupid and offensive, that the Germans did not care what the Italians did about their own interests in Greece and Yugoslavia. He nevertheless chose a moment when Hitler was still recovering from an interview with Franco, in which he had unsuccessfully tried to persuade the Spanish dictator to enter the war against Britain; (the venture had failed because he had been unable to offer the Spanish what they wanted in Africa at the expense of France, for fear of driving the French people and their empire into the arms of de Gaulle).[29] It was in fact questionable whether Italy could hope to profit in this three-cornered haggle over the spoils. But meanwhile, Greece beckoned as a strategic foothold from which to contest German control of the Balkans, to outflank British naval strategy in the eastern Mediterranean, and to expel the British from their most important remaining observation point in Europe.[30]

The whole question was one of man power. Ciano was convinced that Visconti Prasca, who alone of Italian generals 'had the impetuosity of Rommel, but this was the only quality of Rommel's that he had',[31] would have sufficient troops in Albania to do all the necessary fighting. His confidence did not at first seem unreasonable: the Italians had a two-to-one advantage in infantry, a substantial lead in armour, and a superiority in air power of 400 against 115.[32] But the Greeks had been mobilized ever since 24 August; the Italian armour was never able to break out of the mountain passes into terrain where it could be used effectively; and the Regia Aeronautica found itself operating in unsuitable weather conditions, from hopeless airfields.[33] The offensive, begun on 28 October, had been transformed into a retreat by the end of the month. The march of Italian Fascism through the world was over.

The fighting was not. On 6 November the British counter-offensive in Africa began with an assault on Gallabat, ending five days later with the Italians still holding the village, after their CR42 biplanes had driven the British Gladiator biplanes from the sky, in the last air battle of the First World War.

But the victory of Gallabat lost all significance by comparison with the disaster of Taranto. Twenty-one Swordfish, launched in two waves from the aircraft carrier *Illustrious,* crippled the battleship *Cavour,* and put the two battleships *Duilio* and the brand-new *Littorio,* with nine 15-inch guns, out of action for the next six months. The British had lost two aircraft, but the Italians now had only two battleships left, the old *Cesare,* and the Littorio's sister ship, *Vittorio Veneto.* They could no longer fight a fleet action; they could only hope to survive.

British carriers had won supremacy in the Mediterranean at last. On 13 November the Greeks captured Koritza, thirteen miles within Albania itself, and on 8 December they took Argyrokastro on the southern flank. Then on 9 December Graziani's dangerously exposed 40,000 men east of Sidi Barrani were assailed by a British army of 31,000, led by 275 tanks, including fifty-two of the virtually impregnable Matildas, while eighty-seven Hurricanes drove the old CR42s from the sky. It was all over in a couple of days. With his air force massacred, his armour effectively outnumbered five to one, and his anti-tank weapons useless against the Matildas, Graziani had no chance – 38,114 Italian prisoners were taken, for a total loss to the British forces of 624 killed, wounded and missing.

No battles between modern armies were ever won so cheaply. But their very success carried the seeds of future British defeat. The Germans responded immediately on 10 December, before the Battle of Sidi Barrani was over, by beginning to transfer units of the Luftwaffe to Italian bases. Italy's 'parallel war' in the

Mediterranean was over. The kingdom would have to fight for the rest of the war as a German protectorate.

Graziani's only strategy now was to buy time. The Germans were assembling in Sicily, and two armoured divisions, the Ariete and the Centaurio, were being equipped in Italy for transfer to Africa, supposing there was an Italian foot-hold left on the continent to send them to. But the British were still being delayed by sieges and by the unstinted sacrifice of the Regia Aeronautica. Whereas Graziani had perhaps 300 aircraft in useable condition on 9 December, he had 119 left at most on 5 January 1942, and by 9 January the number was down to 91.[34] Meanwhile, the British offensive swept on. Bardia fell on 7 January, after a siege of sixteen days, and 40,000 men with 400 guns surrendered to a besieging force equipped with 100 guns. British casualties were 456. Tobruk fell fourteen days later, when Petassi Manella and his garrison of 25,000 capitulated after a day's fighting, in which the attackers lost a further 400 men.

Even the German intervention did not immediately improve the prospects for the Italian Empire. By the beginning of 1941, 174 German aircraft had been deployed in Sicily, to strike against the British Mediterranean fleet. They made their presence felt on 10 January, crippling the aircraft carrier *Illustrious* in a dive-bombing attack, while the attention of the British fleet fighters was diverted by Italian torpedo-bombers. However, the British still had the *Eagle* to give some measure of aerial cover to their battle fleet, which bombarded Genoa, Leghorn and Spezia without retaliation, provided artillery support for the main Greek offensive against Valona on 9 February,[35] and swept into the harbour of Tripoli for a spectacular but ineffectual shelling. Meanwhile, aircraft from Malta destroyed twenty-five of the new German arrivals on the ground in Sicily, and the army of the Nile smashed the last Italian units in Cyrenaica, in a battle at Beda Fomm, where the Italians enjoyed for the first time a superiority of four to one in armour.

The situation had finally become intolerable to the Germans. A directive issued by Hitler on 11 February provided that

German troops detached for the recovery of North Africa should serve only under a German commander, who should have the right of appeal to his own high command before carrying out an Italian order which he deemed unpromising. At the same time, German troops assembling in Romania began moves to enter the territory of Italy's dynastic ally, Bulgaria.

But the Italians were still capable of a rally themselves. A British attempt to seize the islands of Kaso and Castelrosso in the Dodecanese on 17 February was effectively beaten off by promptly reinforced Italian garrisons. Then on the night of 25–26 March the most typical and most successful Italian weapon of two World Wars made its triumphant reappearance. An attack by MAS-boats on Alexandria had been planned as early as August 1940, but had been frustrated by the sinking of the mother ship, *Iride,* by British aircraft. A further attempt on Gibraltar in October had proved fruitless. But in March 1941 three MAS penetrated Suda Bay and sank the British heavy cruiser *York* and three merchant ships, without loss to themselves.[36] It was the first victory by a surface vessel of the Italian navy in the Second World War, and it came just in time to afford some consolation for Italy's most crushing naval defeat. On the following night, British batteships sank three Italian cruisers and two destroyers off Cape Matapan. This disaster was followed on 16 April by the sinking of five Italian merchant ships and three destroyers off the Kerkenah Banks by a British cruiser and four destroyers, in an encounter redeemed for the Italians only by the heroism of Captain Cristoforo, who succeeded in sinking the British destroyer *Mohawk* before going down with his own mortally-stricken ship. On 19 May the Italian forces in East Africa surrendered to the British, concluding a campaign which cost the Italians 1,988 European and 16,848 native battle casualties, as well as about 260,000 prisoners, against 6,000 British battle casualties in all.[37]

Nor had any honour been gained by the final occupation of Greece, in the wake of the German offensive, after a struggle which had cost 65,000 Italian and 43,000 Greek casualties, and tied up twenty-one Italian divisions in the defence of Albania.[38] Italian officers noted gloomily that 'after so much bloodshed, so much effort, so much humiliation, Italy found herself relegated to a secondary role':[39] the Greeks even refused to surrender to Italian paratroops who landed in Corfu, insisting on waiting for the Germans before they handed over their weapons.[40]

But some real measure of success was at hand. Even the miserable Balkan campaign had at least provided the Italians with the opportunity to thrust their long standing separatist colleague Ante Pavelić into power in Croatia, before the Germans had time to appoint a pet quisling of their own. Pavelić responded by offering the crown of Croatia to the House of Savoy, a presentation which had to be deferred for the time being, until the frontiers of the proposed kingdom could be agreed upon. Meanwhile, the navy and the Regia Aeronautica were being presented with new opportunities, as the huge German air detachments were moved north, in preparation for the attack on Russia. Responsibility for the Battle of the Convoys was falling increasingly on to Italy's 115 bombers and the heroes of the MAS flotillas. So far, the main reason for the failure of the Regia Aeronautica had been, in the trenchant words of Admiral Hezlet, 'that they never hit with their bombs';[41] but this was no longer quite the case. Torpedo-bomber squadron 281, formed on 28 March, sank four British ships on 2 April and three more during the Battle of Pantellaria, on 14 and 15 June, while the high-level bombers scored their first and only success, sinking the destroyer *Juno* on 23 May. Hitler's invasion of Russia provided Mussolini with another opportunity to utilize the forces he was unable to send to Africa, where they could have saved his empire. In a drearily doctrinaire piece of political analysis, he explained to Hitler how well he understood all the irrelevant reasons for the assault on Russia, at the same time urgently reminding Hitler that Italy 'could not remain on the sideline' in this new conflict.[42] It was duly agreed that a 'Corpo di Spedizioni Italiano in Russia' should be formed, with 60,000 men, 4,000 horses and eighty-three aircraft.[43] This was not exactly going to turn the tide in a conflict in which the combined armies opposed at the outset numbered 300 divisions;

nevertheless, in a desperate bid to impress the Germans, the heroes of MAS 10 were sacrified in a suicidal attack on Valetta harbour 'in the jaws of the wolf'.[44] Eight MAS, a motor-torpedo-boat and two 'human torpedoes' were destroyed by the harbour defences and British aircraft, a defeat of which any navy might be proud.[45] And it had cost Italy many of its best sailors, some of whom had deliberately blown themselves up with their vessels.[46] Still Mussolini continued to importune Hitler with offers of more Italian lives to be squandered in Russia,[47] as the C.S.I.R. rolled on to the Dnieper, in the wake of the German advance.[48]

The offer did not fall on deaf ears. Even Ribbentrop, the least sensitive of diplomats, warned the German authorities in Greece to leave the selection of a Greek puppet government strictly to the Italians.[49] And in Bucharest secret talks began between the Italian Minister, Baron Scoppa, and Romania's Antonescu, on the formation of a 'Latin Axis' of Italy, France, Spain, Portugal and Romania to contain German expansion and Slav impulsiveness. Hitler replied warmly and courteously to a further plea from Mussolini that the exhaustion of its reserves of oil had made large-scale employment of the Italian navy impossible: he referred respectfully to the performance of Italian airmen in the convoy battle of 27 September, when Sergeant Valetti, on his first and last combat mission, plunged suicidally into the British fleet, to distract attention from the torpedo-bombers.[50] However, the Fuehrer could promise to help Italy only as much as humanly possible, pointing out the demands of the Russian Blitzkrieg on available oil supplies.[51] Mussolini responded by arguing again that Italy was only making a 40 per cent contribution to the war effort of the Axis, and that it was unjust that his country should not be able to wage war on a scale commensurate with its demographic resources.[52]

Italy's inability to send its alleged eight million bayonets where they were most wanted was made all too obvious on 18 November, when the British went over to the offensive again in North Africa, deploying 1,072 front-line aircraft against 304

Italian and 150 German, and 724 tanks against 308 Italian and 249 German.[53] Within a month, the Axis forces had been thrown back again to the frontiers of Tripolitania. Then during the night of 18–19 December the balance of naval power in the Mediterranean was altered entirely. At 9 p.m., the Italian submarine *Scire* dropped three large, electrically powered 'human torpedoes' outside Alexandria, each carrying two men. Luck was for once on the Italians' side. When the nets protecting the harbour were opened to permit the entry of returning British destroyers, the Italians rode in behind their enemies, as their predecessors had done with the Austrian battle fleet in 1918. Working half blinded in the mud beneath the British battleship *Valiant,* Lieutenant Durande de la Penne, whose brother had sacrified himself in the attack on Valetta, attached a warhead to it by main strength. Vicenzo Martellotta did the same to the fleet tanker *Sagona,* and Antonio Marceglia to the battleship *Queen Elizabeth.*[54] Their success was total. All three ships sank at their moorings, and the British no longer had a battleship in the Mediterranean.

It was revenge for Taranto, and it was followed by a rise in prestige on every front. The arrival of a convoy in Tripoli, escorted by the Italian battle fleet, made possible Rommel's successful riposte on 5 January 1942. On the following day the victory of the C.S.I.R. in the Battle of Christmas on the Russian front was recognized by its being reconstituted as the Armata Italiana in Russia with 227,000 men, 1,300 tanks and 960 guns, though with only fifty-two effective anti-tank guns. Italy thus became Germany's fourth most important ally in Russia, providing ten divisions to supplement the thirteen Hungarian, fourteen Finnish, 15 Romanian and 170 German.[55] In the air, the Macchi M202 and the Regianne Re2001 were at last able to meet at least second-rate British aircraft on reasonably equal terms, even though the incurably irrational Italian aircraft industry went on turning out the long-obsolete CR42 and the wholly unsuccessful Breda G50 in even larger numbers than the desperately needed new Macchis.[56] This military resurgence naturally attracted some diplomatic recognition. Horthy's President of the Council, Kallay, discussed tentatively with Mussolini during March the prospects of taking up the old idea of a 'Latin Front', this time in the form of a 'Balkan Front', consisting of Italy, Hungary and Romania, with the possible participation of Greece and even Turkey. Mussolini stalled for time, however, waiting for even more impressive military victories to strengthen his hand in dealing with Hitler.[57]

He lost the opportunity, even though the successes were still coming. On 26 May Rommel resumed the offensive in Libya with a predominantly Italian army,[58] and by 14 June the Italians had at last managed to earn a substantial share of the credit for an almost complete air-sea victory over the British. In separate engagements 192 Italian aircraft and Admiral de Zara's squadron of two cruisers and five destroyers, unfruitfully supported by Admiral Iachino's battle fleet of two battleships, six cruisers and twelve destroyers, joined with forty German aircraft and a few E-boats. They launched their attack on two British convoys numbering seventeen merchant ships in all, escorted by a battleship, two aircraft carriers, eleven cruisers and forty-three destroyers, and supported by about seventy-five sea- and land-based aircraft. The ensuing mêlées cost the British one destroyer sunk by a mine, two destroyers and two merchant ships sunk by German aircraft, one cruiser sunk by a German submarine, a destroyer sunk by a German E-boat, one merchant ship sunk by Italian aircraft and two merchant ships actually sunk by the guns of da Zara's squadron, which also crippled a British destroyer, leaving it to be finished off by the Regia Aeronautica. One Italian cruiser was sunk by a British submarine.[59]

It was perhaps a German rather than an Italian triumph, though no one could have denied da Zara the satisfaction of bringing his ships back to Naples, with their guns elevated skywards, in token of victory.[60] It was after all the only occasion in the Second World War on which the guns of the Italian fleet actually sank anything. Meanwhile, MAS transported overland to Helsinki were distinguishing themselves in the siege of Leningrad, while fourteen MAS in the Black Sea crippled Russian seaborne traffic there, and sank a Russian cruiser and submarine for a loss of one of their own number.[61] At this high peak of Italian gratification, Mussolini flew to Tripoli on 29 June, to be on hand for the triumphal entry into Alexandria and the recapture of the Italian Empire. But Rommel was halted at El Alamein on 2 July, and eighteen days later Mussolini had to return to Rome. Fifty-two years of history had come to an end. Italy's bid for greatness was over.

There was still to be one final blaze of glory. On 10 August another huge British convoy of fourteen merchant ships, escorted by two battleships, three aircraft carriers, seven cruisers, and twenty-four destroyers, set out in a bid to relieve Malta, already on the point of collapse. Using every possible means of aerial attack, German aircraft sank three merchant ships, and Italian one merchant ship and a destroyer. Again it was the Italian navy that made the biggest contribution: on the night of 12 August Italian submarines sank another merchantman and a cruiser, and produced the conditions of chaos most propitious for an attack by MAS. Eight Italian and two German vessels made the assault. It was almost the last charge of the MAS, the last victory of Italy at sea, the last defeat of Britain, with four more merchant ships and another British cruiser sent to the bottom by the hurtling MAS. An intervention by the big ships of the Italian fleet at this stage could have saved the war for the Axis. Global victory was one torpedo away. But the Italians would not stir without air cover, and the Luftwaffe and the Regia Aeronautica, peeved at their own unsatisfactory showing, insisted on keeping all their available aircraft for a final effort themselves. The battle of mid-August had been won, but the war had been lost.[62]

Malta was relieved. The irresistible British build-up in Egypt continued. Only in Russia the Germans continued to advance rapidly in the south, leaving the Hungarians, Romanians and Italians holding a dangerously extended defensive line north of Voronezh. The game was soon played out. On 31 August at Alam-Halfa, Rommel lost his bid for victory in Africa and on

10 October the German offensive in Russia was effectively halted. Fourteen days later the British attacked at El Alamein, with eighty-six battalions against forty-two Italian and twenty-eight German; 939 guns against 371 Italian and 200 German; and 1,348 tanks against 259 Italian and 238 German.[63] Appeals from the army for more supplies drew the hopeless response from Mussolini's Chief of Staff, Cavallero, that the Italian navy was unable to act from lack of fuel. For twenty-four hours, between 5 and 6 November, Mussolini dallied with the idea of a separate peace but the Germans and the march of events alike gave him no time to prepare himself for a decision which he was on all evidence incapable of making. In any case, plans had already been drafted in October for German and Italian intervention in France if the situation in North Africa deteriorated. Then on 8 November began the Anglo-American landings in French Africa, on the following day, units of the Luftwaffe and the Regia Aeronautica started to arrive in Tunisia, and the occupation of France followed within forty-eight hours. But even as attempts were being made to stabilize the front in Africa, the Russians completed the encirclement of the German forces in front of Stalingrad. Again Mussolini reflected on the possibility of getting out. But 11 December saw the Russians break through the Hungarian-Romanian-Italian line between Voronezh and Orel, deploying forces with a superiority of four to one in men, and nine to one in armour. Losses among the allies were enormously increased by the fact that the German troops on that sector of the front decamped with the available transport, as they had done at El Alamein, leaving their co-belligerents with no option but to surrender. Meanwhile, Rommel abandoned Agheila and continued to fall back on Tripoli. In a sudden flash of insight, German Chief of Staff Keitel appealed to Mussolini, declaring that the outcome of the war now depended on the Italian navy,[64] a conclusion which would have been perfectly true at any time during the past two years. But the only function that the navy could perform now was to expend its last ships and last reserves of fuel in suicidal missions of supply to reinforce

the German and Italian divisions assembling in Tunisia.[65]

Germany's other allies at least knew where they should stand. Demoralized, defeated and almost helpless, Italy's diplomatic importance to the East Europeans ironically increased with the diminishing prospects of Axis victory. Visions of a Latin Community became more important than ever to an area threatened with a Russian domination incalculable in its extent. Romania's Antonescu remarked on 10 January that Italy had become 'the only point of support' for the Balkans in the gathering storm. Mussolini could only comment dully that Italy would march with Germany to the end. Hungary's Regent Horthy renewed the attack on 14 January. His country, which had been Italy's oldest ally, had been ostentatiously neglected by its partner ever since the Hungarians had ignored Mussolini's recommendation in mid-1941 that they should stay out of the war with Russia, on the grounds that it was a matter not affecting Eastern Europe directly.[66] Trade between the two countries had nevertheless tripled during 1942,[67] and Kallay had made unappreciated suggestions in March of that year about taking up Mussolini's own idea of a 'Latin Front', even offering the throne of Hungary to the House of Savoy in August as Pavelić had previously offered that of Croatia. He now affirmed that a common front with Italy was Hungary's only anchor in a German-Slav sea.

Mussolini had other things on his mind, however. Tripoli was evacuated on 23 January. The empire had now gone completely, apart from Albania and the Dodecanese. Eight days later, the German defence at Stalingrad collapsed. On 5 February Mussolini reorganized his government; again took charge of Foreign Affairs himself; and considered grimly the possibilities of persuading Hitler to accept 'the Italian point of view . . . defensive on the Eastern Front and the primary importance of the Mediterranean theatre'.[68] The results were not encouraging, for the Germans remained committed to the notion of an offensive war in the East. Meanwhile, the Turks began cautiously raising with the Bulgarian government of King Boris, as well as with the Greek and Yugoslav governments-in-exile, the notion of a Balkan Federation, naturally under Turkish leadership, and existing for the main purpose of keeping the Russians away from the Mediterranean.[69] German pressure apparently managed to dissuade Boris from co-operating with what to a Balkan leader could scarcely have been an attractive notion, but Mussolini in his turn was assailed by new proposals from Horthy, who pointed out that the Croats were starting to draw away from their Axis partners; that the Germans were not responsive; and that Italy, Finland and Hungary should accordingly adopt a policy separate from that of Hitler. Mussolini yet again rejected the notion of a separate peace;[70] what he did was to instruct his ambassador in Madrid to investigate the possibilities of Franco's being prepared to mediate between Italy and the United Nations.[71] But Franco had no intention of getting involved.[72] The collapse of Axis fortunes continued. Even when Tunis fell to the Anglo-Americans on 12 May, the Hungarians hopelessly renewed their determination to 'cling tight to Italy' whatever happened.[73] The Romanians in equal despair raised a hope that Salazar of Portugal might be induced to mediate on behalf of the Latin satellites, even when Franco had declined to do so, but they reserved their own right to seek a separate peace as soon as possible after the Russians had reached the Dnieper.[74]

To all this Mussolini could only repeat that Italy would conquer or fall at the side of Germany. But talk of military action on Italy's part no longer made any sense; it was even something of a miracle that the country was still in the war at all. The simple truth was that, cut off from all European or non-European sources of supply except Germany, Italian industry had foundered from sheer deprivation.[75] Industrial production was 43 per cent below the level of 1939, and 28 per cent below that of 1928. Production of fuel had fallen from 3,129,000 tons in 1939 to 1,500,000 tons; of iron, from 1,000,000 tons to 231,000 tons; and of steel, from 2,283,000 tons to 1,000,000.[76] In March 1943, Italy produced 100 tanks and 400 aircraft; the Germans, 600 and 1,500 respectively; the British, 800 and 2,700; and the Russians 1,500 of each.[77] Italian shipyards, with a capacity for construction of 400,000 tons of shipping in a year, had built only 263,670 tons in three years of war.[78] In consequence of this the merchant marine had fallen in size from 3 million to 300,000 tons,[79] and the cost of living in Italy had risen by 169 per cent.[80] The average Italian was subsisting on 1,100 calories a day, a diet little more than half that available to the Germans, and only slightly more than that received by the cruelly oppressed Poles. It had been a long and dreadful road from Stresa.

It had to be the end. Mussolini had no longer the will or the constitution to be other than the helpless disciple of Hitler. On 10 July the Anglo-Americans landed in Sicily, materially assisted by the Mafia, and with a superiority of three to one in tanks and guns, and four to one in aircraft.[81] A fortnight later Mussolini was dismissed from office by King Victor Emmanuel, on the authority of the Fascist Grand Council, and replaced by Marshal Badoglio. Plans were prepared to close the Brenner against further German troop movements. But there were eight German divisions on Italian territory already, two of which were in a position to counter any Italian attempt to block the passes. Seven more German divisions arrived within a fortnight. Badoglio nevertheless began preliminary soundings with the British minister at the Vatican on 30 July, three days after he had assured the Germans of his determination to continue the war. Precious time was wasted by the insistence of the British and Americans on the technicalities of 'unconditional surrender'; in any event, Badoglio feared the consequences of German retaliation if he announced the surrender before an Allied landing; and the Allied leaders feared to make the landing without first being assured that the Italians had surrendered. It was therefore not until 3 September that the first Anglo-American forces crossed the Straits of Messina. On 7 September the German high command took the decision to disarm all Italian units as a safety measure, being quickly assured by King Victor Emmanuel on the following day that Italy would never be false to the German alliance. On 8 September Badoglio announced the decision to surrender.

Italy was by no means out of the war, however. The navy and

the Regia Aeronautica still had a chance of escaping from German vengeance, even after a surprise attack by the Luftwaffe sank the brand-new battleship *Roma,* while it was leading the Italian navy to Valetta. Thirty-two divisions of soldiers were cut off by the Germans in the Balkans and forced to surrender, after some desperate fighting in Montenegro, Albania, Greece and the Aegean. Meanwhile, Badoglio took the Royal Family out of Rome before the Germans completed occupying the city, and established his government in Brindisi, from where he declared war on Germany on 13 October, thus providing an example to be followed by the Romanian government of King Michael in the following August. But Latin diplomacy no longer existed. King Boris of Bulgaria had already died, in the most suspicious circumstances possible, after an unsatisfactory interview with the Germans; his successors had hoped to declare war against Germany at the same time as Romania, but were literally given no time to do so by the speed of the Russian advance. Only the indefatigable Hungarians preserved to the end the last glimmer of inter-war Mediterranean diplomacy, persisting in recognizing the royal government in the south of Italy, as well as Mussolini's puppet régime in the north.

Italian influence in the Mediterranean was past fighting for, but Italian military honour was not. The contribution made to the United Nations by Badoglio's Italy of the Armistice was by no means merely formal: 315 Italian aircraft flew 9,444 missions of combat or supply between 8 September 1943 and July 1944; the Italian army provided the United Nations with 330,000 men for various duties, including four full combat divisions, which performed impressively at Monte Longo in December, and subsequently in the campaigns of May 1944.[82] Over 17,000 of Italy's 77,500 combat dead fell in the battles of the liberation.

It had nevertheless been an appallingly unsuccessful war for the Italians. No Great Power, except perhaps Austria after the First World War, ever had to look back on a military experience quite so massively discouraging. Only occasionally in Russia had the army won a significant victory without suffering totally uneconomic losses. The Regia Aeronautica had lost 6,483 aircraft, against 1,920 enemy planes destroyed. The navy had lost to enemy action in the Mediterranean two battleships, fourteen cruisers, sixty-three destroyers and escort vessels, eighty-four submarines and fifty MAS – of these, both battleships, six cruisers and twenty-six destroyers had been lost to air attacks; three cruisers and twelve destroyers had been torpedoed by submarines; nineteen destroyers or escorts had run into mines; and five cruisers and sixteen destroyers had been sunk in surface actions with the British. Royal Navy losses by contrast amounted to two battleships, eight cruisers or auxiliaries, eleven destroyers and forty-one submarines. Two of the destroyers and one cruiser had been lost to Italian aircraft; four cruisers and two destroyers had been sunk by submarines; a cruiser and four destroyers had hit mines; both battleships, two cruisers and a destroyer had been sunk by MAS; and only two British destroyers had actually succumbed to action by major surface units of the Italian navy.[83] The MAS and the submarines had very nearly done it all by themselves.

There was every reason for the Italians' lack of success. The Regia Aeronautica had never had a chance to regain the technological lead which it had established in the years of peace, and which it had been unable to sustain under the pressure of the Abyssinian and Spanish campaigns, followed so closely as they were by involvement in the Second World War. Italian aircraft were too few, too slow and too lightly armed; they lacked armour, reliable radios and equipment for night flying.[84] The navy lacked radar, training in night action, and adequate air cover, and in the last two years of the war it even lacked fuel.[85] It was also handicapped by an official policy which forbade it to seek action except when it was certain of an easy victory, which under the circumstances it never could be, and of which the only justification is that there was at least a sufficient number of ships left in September 1943 to make their surrender diplomatically worth while.

Defeat stemmed from the fatal year 1935, and could have

been predicted then. But Italy was not entirely to blame for not having predicted it. Churchill hypocritically condemned Mussolini for the decision to enter the war on the side of Nazi Germany in 1940, while lauding him for his achievement in raising Italy to a position of influence which it had never enjoyed before.[86] But the decision for war had been taken in the expectation of an imminent Germany victory, at a time when few unbiased observers outside the United Kingdom could reasonably have expected anything else. Entry into a war which Germany had embarked on three years ahead of schedule was the only way in which Italy could hope to ensure that a post-war settlement might reflect something more than purely German interest. It was certainly the only way in which Italy could hope to secure the share of the French Empire which had been its price for neutrality or even alliance with the West in 1939. The Pact of Steel had always been for the Fascists primarily a means of containing German ambitions in central and eastern Europe. The decision for war was the only way of making that containment effective.

It was a strategy that came so close to working that one cannot in all logic condemn it. The Second World War was won by the narrowest possible of margins. For ten days in September Germany was winning the Battle of Britain; Japan was within two minutes of winning the Battle of Midway; Italy was one torpedo away from victory in the Mediterranean in July 1942.

For the Second World War was rendered possible only by Mussolini's decision to invade Abyssinia, and the decision of the British government to make a bid for electoral support by opposing that invasion with deliberately ineffectual sanctions. It was a course of action which could have been entertained only by men who believed in parliamentary success rather than in the League of Nations, which they had ignored at the time of the Manchurian crisis; in the independence of Abyssinia, which they would not risk anything to defend; or in the system of Europe, which they were prepared to disregard, to the extent that they were unaware that it existed. The only policy which could have been even more disastrously short-sighted was that of people like Churchill, who were apparently prepared to go to war with Italy, and thus drive the whole of Eastern Europe into the arms of Germany. And this was what eventually happened, but it had not been made inevitable by the men of 1935. Bridges between Italy and the West could have been repaired but for the unanticipated and irreparable misfortune of the Spanish Civil War. An accord was perhaps still possible even in 1939, but only at a price that the French refused to pay. Paris in 1939 refused to sacrifice a province to save an empire, just as Vienna had done in 1915.

Italy has its true existence only as the balancing agent in a system of independent and mutually self-respecting European states, and it was to preserve some shadow of that system that Italy went to war in 1940. Its total collapse in 1943 heralded the extinction of anything that could be called a system of Europe, because for the next two decades, the nations of the Continent, with a few honourable exceptions, endured a kind of diplomatic colonialism without foreign policies of their own, except as prescribed for them by alien Superpowers. It is at least appropriate that the re-emergence of West European nationalism has coincided with the reappearance of Italy as the country which is once again making the system of Europe a reality, by leading the movement to bring the United Kingdom into the Common Market. Twenty-eight years after the holocaust of 1943, Italy has emerged as the Power with the most dynamic economy in Western Europe, the second largest military establishment, the third largest population, and the fourth largest output of goods and services. The future of the Continent depends again, as it depended on so many occasions in the past eighty years, on the manner in which Italy responds to the inevitable call to greatness.

References

CHAPTER ONE

1 *Foreign Relations of the United States*, Marsh to Fish, 21 September 1870
2 *Annual Register of World Events*, 1825, p. 142
3 L. S. Stavrianos, *The Balkans since 1453*, Winston, New York, p. 133
4 D. Mathew, *Ethiopia: the study of a polity*, Eyre and Spottiswoode, London, 1947, p. 131
5 S. Rubenson, 'Aspects of the survival of Ethiopian independence 1840–96' *University College Review*, Addis Ababa, 1961, pp. 253–269
6 R. Battaglia, *La Prime Guerra d'Africa*, Einaudi, Rome, 1958, p. 58
7 E. B. Potter and Chester W. Nimitz, *Sea Power*, Prentice-Hall, New Jersey, 1961, p. 328
8 *Annual Register of World Events*, 1868, p. 140
9 Raffaele Ciasca, *Storia Coloniale dell'Italia Contemporanea*, Hoepli, Milan, 1940, p. 11
10 *Ibid.*, p. 19
11 D. A. Farnie, *East and West of Suez*, O.U.P., 1968, p. 136
12 Alan Moorhead, *The White Nile*, Hamilton, London, 1961, p. 188
13 Battaglia, *op. cit.*, p. 136
14 P. M. Holt, *The Mahdist State in the Sudan, 1881–1898*, Clarendon Press, Oxford, 1958, p. 22
15 J. Grant, *Cassell's History of the War in the Sudan*, Cassell, London, 1887, p. 148
16 *Ibid.*, p. 149
17 Czeslaw Jesman, *The Russians in Ethiopia: An Essay in Futility*, Chatto and Windus, London, 1958, pp. 21–22
18 Jesman, *op. cit.*, p. 15
19 Jesman, *op. cit.*, pp. 43–45
20 Barclay, 'Strange Bedfellows', *Europe in the Twentieth Century*, MacDonald, London, 1970, vol. I, 1900–1914, pp. 132–135
21 Farni, *op. cit.*, p. 432
22 'The Times', *History of the South African War*, London, 1912, vol. VI, p. 267
23 Battaglia, *op. cit.*, p. 639
24 *Ibid.*, p. 739

25 V. Giglio – A. Ravenni, *Le Guerre Coloniale d'Italia*, Casa Editrice, Milan, 1935, p. 329
26 R. Oliver and A. Atmore, *Africa Since 1800*, Cambridge University Press, 1967, p. 184

CHAPTER TWO

1 *Whittaker's Almanac*, 1900, p. 712
2 Francesco Crispi, *Memoirs*, Holder and Stoughton, London, 1912, vol. II, pp. 449–50
3 *Ibid.*, p. 451
4 C. Lapworth, *Tripoli and Young Italy*, Swift, London, 1912, p. 121
5 Ciasca, *op. cit.*, p. 339
6 *Annual Register*, 1900, pp. 378–381
7 *Documents Diplomatiques Français*, (1870–1914), 2 VI, 222
8 L. Albertini, *The Origins of the First World War*, O.U.P., 1965, vol. I, p. 153
9 Albertini, *op. cit.*, vol. I, pp. 193–194
10 Albertini, *op. cit.*, vol. I, pp. 264–265
11 May, A. J., *The Hapsburg Monarchy 1867–1914*, Harvard University Press, 1951, pp. 221–222
12 *Ibid.*, p. 298
13 W. W. Gottlieb, *Studies in Secret Diplomacy During the First World War*, Allen and Unwin, London, 1957, p. 157
14 Albertini, *op. cit.*, vol. I, p. 344
15 *Il Primo Vol di Guerra Nel Mondo*, Stato Maggiore del'Aeronautica Militare, Ministerio Difese Aeronautica, Rome, 1950, p. 77
16 *SMAM*, *op. cit.*, pp. 29–30
17 General A. A. Felice Porro, *La Guerra Nell'Aria*, Corbaccio, Milan, 1935, p. 22
18 Laurence, Lafore, *The Long Fuse*, Lippincott, 1965, p. 169
19 *The Times*, 22 April 1912
20 L. Villari, *The Expansion of Italy*, Faber and Faber, London, 1930, p. 97
21 G. Baer, *The Coming of the Italo-Ethiopian War*, Harvard University Press, 1967, p. 45
22 Seton-Watson, *op. cit.*, p. 377
23 Ciasca, *op. cit.*, p. 384
24 *Documents Diplomatiques Français*, 3, III, 274
25 *Documents Diplomatiques Français*, 3 IV, 108
26 *Annual Register*, 1915, p. 254
27 Villari, *op. cit.*, pp. 99–100
28 L. Mondini, *Prologo del Conflitto Italo-Greco*, Treves, Rome, 1945, pp. 76–78
29 A. Salandra, *Italy and the Great War*, Arnold, London, 1932, p. 33
30 Gottlieb, *op. cit.*, p. 157

31 Sir Josiah Stamp, *Studies in Current Problems in Finance and Government*, King, London, 1924, p. 332
32 *L'Industria Italiana alla Meta Del Secolo xx*, Confederazione Generale dell'Industria Italiana, Rome, 1953, p. 6
33 *Ibid.*, p. 11
34 *Ibid.*, p. 8
35 Stamp, *op. cit.*
36 Albertini, *op. cit.*, vol. I, pp. 221–222
37 Albertini, *op. cit.*, vol. II, p. 18
38 Taylor, *The Struggle for Mastery in Europe 1848–1918*, Clarendon Press, Oxford, 1957, p. 520
39 May, *op. cit.*, p. 298
40 Conrad, III, p. 256
41 Salandra, *op. cit.*, p. 16
42 Salandra, *op. cit.*, pp. 38–41
43 Albertini *op. cit.*, vol. II, p. 132
44 Albertini, *op. cit.*, vol. II, p. 222
45 Albertini, *op. cit.*, p. 311
46 Albertini, *op. cit.*, vol. III, p. 277
47 Albertini, *op. cit.*, p. 283
48 *Ibid.*
49 Austrian Foreign Office, *Documents on the Origins of the War of 1914*, III, p. 80
50 Conrad, IV, p. 194
51 *Documenti Diplomatici Italiani*, 5, I, 65, p. 37
52 Villari, *op. cit.*, p. 138
53 Salandra, *op. cit.*, p. 125
54 Salandra, *op. cit.*, p. 224

CHAPTER THREE

1 General Rodolfo Corselli, *La Grande Guerra Alla Fronti Italia*, 66, Zanichelli, Bologna, 1942, vol. II, p. 45
2 Corselli, *supra*
3 C. Manfroni, *Storia della Marina Italiana dovente la Guerra Mondiale*, Zanichelli, Bologna, 1942, pp. 370–375
4 Commandante Guido Po, *La Guerra Marittima dell'Italia*, Corbaccio, Milan, 1933, p. 45
5 M. Caraccioco, *L'Italia e i suoi Alleati Nella Grande Guerra*, Mondadori, Milan, 1932, p. 43
6 J. F. Edmonds, *A History of World War I*, Longmans, London, 1965, p. 121
7 T. N. Dupuy and M. R. Mayo, *Campaigns in Southern Europe*, Watts, New York, 1967, p. 29
8 John W. R. Taylor, *Combat Aircraft of the World*, Michael Joseph, London, 1970, p. 202

9 Colonel Ettore Grasselli, *L'Esercito Italiano in Francia e in Oriente*, Corbaccio, Milan, 1957, p. 146
10 *Ibid.*, p. 155
11 W. Hubatsch, *Germany and the Central Powers in the World War*, 1914–1918, University of Kansas, Lawrence, 1963, p. 50
12 Confederazione Generale dell'Industria Italiana, *op. cit.*, p. 12
13 Porro, *op. cit.*, p. 25
14 Carlo de Rysky, *I Problemi Della Guerra Moderna e la Politica Militare dell'Italia*, Cisalpino, Milan, 1930, pp. 41–56
15 General V. J. Esposito, *A Concise History of World War I*, Pall Mall, London, 1970 p. 177
16 Caraccioco, *op. cit.*, p. 66
17 Dupuy, *op. cit.*, pp. 47–48
18 De Rysky, *op. cit.*, pp. 41–56
19 Caraccioco, *op. cit.*, p. 74
20 Esposito, *op. cit.*, p. 165
21 Hubatsch, *op. cit.*, p. 59
22 Grasselli, *op. cit.*, p. 305
23 C.R.M.F. Cruttwell, *A History of the Great War, 1914–1918*, Clarendon Press, Oxford, 1934, p. 453
24 Grasselli, *op. cit.*, p. 114
25 Crutwell, *op. cit.*, p. 408
26 Grasselli, *op. cit.*, pp. 121–122
27 L. Salvatorelli and G. Mira, *Storia d'Italia Nel Periodo Fascista*, Finaudi, Turin, 1964, p. 72
28 Edmonds, *op. cit.*, p. 253
29 Dupuy, *op. cit.*, p. 64
30 Mondini, *op. cit.*, p. 65
31 Dupuy, *op. cit.*, 65; Edmonds, *op. cit.*, p. 171; Grasselli, *op. cit.*, p. 65
32 Caraccioco, *op. cit.*, p. 147
33 C. Seton-Watson, *Italy from Liberalism to Fascism, 1870–1925*, Methuen, London, 1967, p. 479
34 Buchan, *op. cit.*, vol. XXI, p. 44
35 *Ibid.*, p. 45
36 Cruttwell, *op. cit.*, p. 465
37 *Ibid.*, p. 464
38 Buchan, *op. cit.*, Appendix I, Sir Henry Plumer's First Despatch of 12 April 1918; Jones, *op. cit.*, Appendix XL; de Rysky, *op. cit.*, pp. 41–56
39 Po, *op. cit.*, p. 290
40 Grasselli, *op. cit.*, p. 33
41 Edmonds, *op. cit.*, p. 282
42 R. W. Seton-Watson, *Europe in the Melting-Pot*, Macmillan, London, 1919, pp. 307–308
43 Dupuy, *op. cit.*, p. 83; Grasselli, *op. cit.*, p. 211
44 Dupuy, *supra*
45 Esposito, *op. cit.*, p. 174

46 *F.R.U.S.*, 1918, Supplt, I, 1, pp. 815–816
47 *Wilson Letters*, 8, 222–223
48 Ivo J. Lederer, *Yugoslavia at the Paris Peace Conference*, Yale, 1963, p. 39
49 Esposito, *op. cit.*, p. 115
50 Grasselli, *op. cit.*, p. 357
51 Despatch 1060 of 1.11.18, cited by de Rysky, *below*
52 De Rysky, *op. cit.*, pp. 41–56
53 F. Paglioni, *Aviatori Italiani*, Longanesi, Milan, 1970, p. 147
54 Lederer, *op. cit.*, p. 40
55 Crutwell, *op. cit.*, pp. 601–602
56 Lederer, *op. cit.*, p. 44
57 General Rodolfo Corselli, *La Grande Guerra Alle Fronti Italiani*, Zanichelli, Bologna, 1942, vol. 2, *passim.* Esposito gives Diaz only fifty-seven divisions (p. 174); Edmonds gives him fifty-eight.
58 *Corriere della Sera*, 30 October 1918
59 Lederer, *op. cit.*, p. 56
60 Po, *op. cit.*, p. 321
61 Lederer, *op. cit.*, p. 56
62 Seton-Watson, *op. cit.*, p. 302
63 Lederer, *op. cit.*, p. 105
64 Lederer, *op. cit.*, pp. 72–75

CHAPTER FOUR

1 Grasselli, *op. cit.*; de Rysky, *op. cit.*; Jones, *op. cit.*, Appendix XXXI
2 Jones, *supra*
3 *Ibid.*; Munson, *op. cit.*, p. 11
4 Lederer, *op. cit.*, p. 137
5 R. Albrecht-Carrie, *Italy at the Peace Conference*, Columbia, New York, 1938, p. 94
6 Seton-Watson, *op. cit.*, pp. 300–301
7 Mondini, *op. cit.*, p. 66
8 Lederer, *op. cit.*, p. 231
9 Lederer, *op. cit.*, p. 233
10 Albrecht-Carrie, *op. cit.*, pp. 254–255
11 Lederer, *op. cit.*, p. 258
12 M. Currey, *Italian Foreign Policy, 1918–1932*, Nicholson and Watson, London, 1932, pp. 52–53
13 Currey, *op. cit.*, p. 57
14 *Corriere della Sera*, 7 August 1920
15 Currey, *op. cit.*, p. 58
16 Barros, *op. cit.*, p. 295
17 Naval Intelligence Division, *op. cit.*, p. 155
18 *Statesman's Yearbook*, 1914 and 1923
19 Villari, *op. cit.*, p. 41
20 C.G.I.I., *op. cit.*, p. 11

21 L. Grebler and W. Winkler, *The Cost of the World War to Germany and to Austria-Hungary*, New Haven, Yale University Press, 1940, pp. 103–104 and pp. 161–163
22 Salvatorelli and Mira, *op. cit.*, pp. 39, 124
23 *Ibid.*, p. 126
24 Seton-Watson, *op. cit.*, p. 569
25 Seton-Watson, *op. cit.*, p. 553
26 Seton-Watson, *op. cit.*, ch. 12, 13 *passim*
27 *Corriere della Sera*, 17 November 1921
28 D.D.1., 7, I, 118
29 *Corriere della Sera*, 16 January 1923
30 J. Barros, *The Corfu Incident of 1923*, Princeton, 1965, p. 34
31 *The Times*, 31 August 1923
32 Royal Institute of International Affairs, *Survey of International Affairs, 1920–1923*, Oxford University Press, 1925, p. 349
33 *Ibid.*
34 *The Times*, 31 August 1923
35 Barros, *op. cit.*, p. 25
36 *The Times*, 5 September 1923
37 Barros, *op. cit.*, p. 180
38 Barros, *op. cit.*, p. 182
39 *Corriere della Sera*, 27 May 1927
40 *The Times*, 16 February 1923
41 M. Missiroli, *Ce Que L'Italie doit a Mussolini*, Edizione di Novissima, Rome, 1938
42 M. Gilbert, *The European Powers, 1900–45*, Plume, 1970, New York, p. 148
43 *R.1.1.A.*, *op. cit.*, pp. 356–357
44 *The Times*, 28 January 1924
45 *Corriere della Sera*, 12 November 1924
46 *The Times*, 7 February 1926
47 Currey, *op. cit.*, p. 173
48 *The Times*, 28 February 1926
49 *Corriere della Sera*, 26 May 1926
50 Articles, I and II
51 *Giornale d'Italia*, 10 December 1926
52 *Whittaker's Almanac*, 1928
53 *C.G.1.1.*, *op. cit.*, p. 11
54 Woytinsky, *op. cit.*, p. 785
55 See p. 136
56 C. A. Macartney, *October Fifteenth: A History of Modern Hungary, 1929–1945*, Edinburgh University Press, 1968, p. 115
57 *Corriere della Sera*, 31 July 1932
58 Baer, *op. cit.*, p. 27
59 E. Wiskemann, *Europe of the Dictators*, Fontana, London, 1966, p. 119
60 Jugoslavia, *op. cit.*, p. 169

61 G. Salveminik, *Prelude to World War II*, Gollancz, London, 1953, pp. 132–133
62 *Ibid.*
63 *Giornale d'Italia*, 10 March 1933
64 Baer, *op. cit.*, p. 27
65 Royal Institute of International Affairs, *Documents on International Affairs*, 1933, pp. 240–249
66 *The Times*, 12 September 1933
67 *Giornale d'Italia*, 24 October 1933
68 R.I.I.A., *Survey of International Affairs, 1934*, Oxford University Press, p. 455; Macintyre, *op. cit.*, p. 144
69 Macintyre, *supra*
70 F. Wiskemann, *The Rome-Berlin Axis*, Fontana, London, 1966, p. 52
71 Wiskemann, *op. cit.*, pp. 53–54
72 *Ibid.*, p. 55
73 Baer, *op. cit.*, p. 41
74 *Corriere della Sera*, 7 September 1934
75 Laurens, *op. cit.*, p. 20
76 Baer, *op. cit.*, ch. 3, *passim*
77 R.I.I.A., *Survey, 1935, op. cit.*, pp. 103–108
78 Baer, *op. cit.*, p. 38
79 Hoptner, *op. cit.*, p. 35
80 R. Guarglia, *Ricordi*, Librarie Plon, Paris, 1955, pp. 214–217
81 Survey, *op. cit.*, p. 136
82 League of Nations, *Official Journal*, May 1935, pp. 569–571
83 *The Times*, 15 April 1935
84 *The Times*, 22 May 1935
85 Baer, *op. cit.*, p. 23
86 L. Pignatelli, *La Guerra dei Seite Mesi*, Editorial Mezzogiorno, Naples, 1940, p. 45
87 *The Times*, 12 September 1935
88 Baer, *op. cit.*, p. 258
89 *Ibid.*, p. 253
90 R.I.I.A., *Survey of International Affairs*, 1936, p. 395
91 A. Williams, *Airpower*, Macmillan, New York, 1937, p. 200
92 J. B. Hoptner, *Yugoslavia in Crisis, 1934–1941*, Columbia University Press, New York, 1963, pp. 46–51
93 M. Missiroli, *Ce Que L'Italie Doit a Mussolini*, Edizione di Novissima, Rome, 1938, p. 208
94 Pignatelli, *op. cit.*, p. 191
95 H. Thomas, *The Spanish Civil War*, Pelican, London, 1968, p. 282
96 *Ibid.*, p. 305
97 *Corriere della Sera*, 2 November 1936
98 Hoptner, *op. cit.*, pp. 95–96
99 C. A. Macartney, *October Fifteenth*, Edinburgh University Press, 1969, vol. 1, pp. 195–196

100 Hoptner, *op. cit.*, p. 81
101 Thomas, *op. cit.*, Appendix 3; *D.G.F.P.*, Series D., IV, p. 518
102 Catalano, *op. cit.*, p. 4
103 Thomas, *op. cit.*, p. 597
104 *Ibid.*, pp. 604–605
105 Wiskemann, *op. cit.*, p. 128
106 *Giornale d'Italia*, 17 March 1938
107 Thomas, *op. cit.*, p. 669
108 M. Toscano, *The Origins of the Pact of Steel*
109 Stavrianos, *op. cit.*, p. 725
110 Ciasca, *op. cit.*, p. 538; Salvatorelli and Mira, *op. cit.*, p. 910
111 *D.G.F.P.*, D, IV, 533
112 Macartney, *op. cit.*, p. 318
113 Hoptner, *op. cit.*, p. 143
114 *Corriere della Sera*, 15 May 1939
115 *D.G.F.P.*, D, IV, 518; Guarglia, *op. cit.*, p. 145; Santoro, *op. cit.*, p. 13
116 Wiskemann, *op. cit.*, pp. 205–206
117 Bocca, *op. cit.*, p. 133
118 Flaccomio, *op. cit.*, p. 71
119 Santoro, *op. cit.*, p. 21
120 Aicker and Evangelisti, *op. cit.*, p. 27
121 Santoro, *supra*, p. 20
122 Fusco, *op. cit.*, p. 12
123 Mondini, *op. cit.*, p. 151
124 *D.D.I.*, 8, XIII, 616–617
125 C.G.I.I., *op. cit.*, p. 26

CHAPTER FIVE

1 W. Churchill, *Their Finest Hour*, The Reprint Society, London, 1954, pp. 87–88
2 General I. S. O. Playfair, *The Mediterranean and the Middle East*, H.M.S.O., London, 1964, vol. 1, pp. 90–92
3 Giorgio Bocca, *Storia d'Italia nella Guerra Fascista*, 1940/3, Laterza, Bari, 1969, p. 133
4 Captain D. McIntyre, *The Battle for the Mediterranean*, Pan, London, 1964, p. 15
5 L. M. Chasson, *Storia Militare della Seconda Guerra*, Mondiale, Sansoni, Florence, 1964, p. 83
6 Chassin, *op. cit.*, p. 91
7 Luigi Mondini, *op. cit.*, p. 262
8 Bocca, *op. cit.*, p. 211
9 Playfair, *op. cit.*, p. 118
10 Bocca, *op. cit.*, p. 170
11 Salvatorelli and Mira, *op. cit.*, p. 1044

12 Santoro, *op. cit.*, p. 127
13 *Ibid.*, pp. 135–136
14 Bocca, *op. cit.*, p. 237
15 Playfair, *op. cit.*, p. 149
16 F. Paglioni, *Aviatori Italiani*, Longanesi, Milan, 1970, pp. 11–12
17 F. Faldella, *L'Italia e La Seconda Guerra Mondiale*, Cappelli, Rome, 1969, p. 122
18 Macintyre, *op. cit.*, p. 30
19 Santoro, *op. cit.*, p. 342
20 Flaccomio, *op. cit.*, p. 147
21 General A. Kindelan, *La Guerra en el Mediterraneo y el Norte de Africa*, Idea, Madrid, 1965, p. 70
22 Documents on German Foreign Policy, *Series D*, vol. X, no. 353
23 Playfair, *op. cit.*, p. 195
24 M. Aicker and Giorgio Evangelisti, *Storia degli Aerosiluranti Italiani*, Longanesi, Milan, 1970, pp. 19, 27
25 Guarglia, *op. cit.*, p. 177
26 J. D. Brown, *Carrier Operations in World War II*, vol. I: *The Royal Navy*, Ian Allan, London, 1968, p. 75
27 Chassin, *op. cit.*, p. 83
28 Wiskemann, *op. cit.*, p. 275
29 Wiskemann, *op. cit.*
30 Mondini, *op. cit.*, p. 182
31 M. Cervi, *Storia della Guerra di Grecia*, Sugar Editore, Milan, 1965, p. 274
32 *Ibid.*, p. 140
33 Santoro, *op. cit.*, pp. 160, 225
34 Paglioni, *op. cit.*, p. 75
35 Cervi, *op. cit.*, p. 243
36 J. Borghese, *Decima Flottiglia MAS*, Garzanti, Rome, 1968, pp. 97–103
37 Chassin, *op. cit.*, p. 91
38 Cervi, *op. cit.*, p. 373
39 *Ibid.*, p. 321
40 *Ibid.*, pp. 363–364
41 Vice-Admiral Sir Arthur Hezlet, *Aircraft and Sea Power*, Peter Davies, London, 1970, p. 163
42 Mussolini to Hitler, D.G.F.P., 23 June 1941
43 F. Valori, *Gli Italiani in Russia*, Bieti, Milan, 1967, p. 43
44 Borghese, *op. cit.*, p. 138
45 *Ibid.*
46 Bocca, *op. cit.*, p. 394
47 Macintyre, *op. cit.*, p. 127
48 D.G.F.P., *Series D*, vol. IV, 421; Valori, *op. cit.*, p. 45
49 D.G.F.P., *Series D*, vol. IV
50 *Ibid.*, 421; Paglioni, *op. cit.*, p. 51
51 D.G.F.P., *Series D*, vol. IV, 431

52 *Ibid.*, 454
53 Faldella, *op. cit.*, p. 233
54 E. Stafford, *The Far and the Deep*, Barker, London, 1968, p. 265
55 Valori, *op. cit.*, p. 242; B. Crespi, *La Battaglia di Natale*, Longanesi, Milan, 1965, pp. 154–158
56 G. Lazzati, *I Soliti Quattro Galli*, Marsia, Milan, 1965, p. 46
57 Fadella, *op. cit.*, pp. 329–330
58 *Ibid.*, p. 260
59 Peter Smith, *Pedestal*, Kimber, London, 1971, pp. 22-30
60 P. Shankland and A. Hunter, *Malta Convoy*, Fontana, London, 1969, p. 61
61 Valori, *op. cit.*, p. 384
62 Peter Smith, *Pedestal*, Kimber, London, 1971, *passim*
63 Fadella, *op. cit.*, p. 291
64 F. W. Deakin, *The Brutal Friendship*, Weidenfeld and Nicholson, London, 1962, p. 102
65 Macintyre, *op. cit.*, pp. 211–217
66 Macartney, *op. cit.*, vol. II, p. 25
67 *Ibid.*, p. 58
68 Deakin, *op. cit.*, p. 193
69 *Ibid.*, pp. 252–253
70 Macartney, *op. cit.*, vol. II, p. 147
71 Deakin, *supra*, p. 293
72 *Ibid.*
73 *Ibid.*, p. 307
74 Guarglia, *op. cit.*, p. 301
75 Catalano, *op. cit.*, p. 26
76 *Ibid.*
77 Bocca, *op. cit.*, p. 505
78 C.G.I.T., *op. cit.*, p. 32
79 *Ibid.*
80 Bocca, *supra*, p. 447
81 Bocca, *op. cit.*, p. 553
82 Fadella, *op. cit.*, p. 394
83 S. W. Roskill, *op. cit.*, vol. III, part 1, appendix G
84 Guarglia, *op. cit.*, p. 177; Santoro, *op. cit.*, p. 20
85 Macintyre, *op. cit.*, p. 112
86 W. S. Churchill, *Closing the Ring*, The Reprint Society, 1954, pp. 57–58

Bibliography

OFFICIAL SOURCES AND WORKS OF REFERENCE

Annual Register of World Events, 1825, 1868, 1900, 1915
Documenti Diplomatici Italiani
Documents Diplomatiques Francais, 1870–1914
Documents on German Foreign Policy
Foreign Relations of the United States
H. A. Jones, *The War in the Air*, O.U.P., London, 1937
Playfair, Major-General I. S. O. *The Mediterranean and the Middle East*, H.M.S.O., London, 1964
Po, Commandante Guido. *La Guerra Marittima dell'Italia*, Corbaccio, Milan, 1963
Porro, General A. A. Felice. *La Guerra Nell'Aria*, Corbaccio, Milan, 1939
Roskill, Captain S. W. *The War at Sea*, H.M.S.O., London, 1960
Royal Institute of International Affairs, *Documents on International Affairs, 1933*, O.U.P., London, 1935
Statesman's Yearbook, 1916, 1923
Stato Maggiore del'Aeronautica Militare, *Il Primo Vol di Guerra Nel Mondo*, Ministerio Difese Aeronautica, Rome, 1950
Whittaker's Alamanac, 1900, 1928

NEWSPAPERS

Corriere della Sera
Giornale d'Italia
The Times

OTHER SOURCES

Aicker, M. and Evangelisti, G. *Storia degli Aerosiluranti Italiani*, Longanesi, Milan, 1970
Albertini, L. *The Origins of the First World War*, O.U.P., London, 1965
Albrecht-Carrie, R. *Italy at the Peace Conference*, Columbia U.P., New York, 1938

Baer, G. W. *The Coming of the Italian-Ethiopian War*, Harvard U.P., Cambridge, 1967

Barros, J. *The Corfu Incident of 1923*, Princeton U.P., 1965

Battaglia, R. *La Prima Guerra d'Africa*, Einaudi, Rome, 1958

Bernotti, Admiral *La Guerra sul Mare nel Conflitto Mondiale, 1939–1941*, Terrina, Livorno, 1966

Bocca, G. *Storia d'Italia nella Guerra Fascista, 1940–1943*, Laterza Bari, 1969

Borghese, J. *Decima Flottiglia M.A.S.*, Garzanti, Rome, 1968

Brown, J. D. *Carrier Operations in World War II: The Royal Navy*, Ian Allan, London, 1968

Buchan, J. *Nelson's History of the War*, Thomas Nelson and Sons, London, 1914–1920

Caraccioco, M. *L'Italia e i suoi Alleati Nella Grande Guerra*, Mondadori, Milan, 1932

Catalano, F. *L'Economia Italiana di Guerra, 1935–1943*, Instituto Nazionale per la Sturia del Movimento di Liberazione, Florence, 1969

Cervi, M. *Storia della Guerra di Grecia*, Sugar Editore, Milan, 1965

Chassin, L. M. *Storia Militare della Secondo Guerra Mondiale*, Sansoni, Florence, 1964

Churchill, W. S. *Their Finest Hour*, The Reprint Society, London, 1954

Churchill, W. S. *Closing the Ring*, The Reprint Society, London, 1954

Ciasca, R. *Storia Coloniale dell'Italia Contemporanea*, Hoepli, Milan, 1940

Confederazione Generale dell'Industria Italiana, *L'Industria Italiana alla Meta del Secolo XX*, Rome, 1953

Corselli, General R. *La Grande Guerra Alla Fronti Italiani*, Zanichelli, Bologna, 1942

Crispi, F. *Memoirs*, Hodder and Stoughton, London, 1912

Crutwell, C. R. M. F. *A History of the Great War, 1914–1918*, Clarendon, Oxford, 1934

Currey, M. *Italian Foreign Policy, 1918–1932*, Nicholson and Watson, London, 1932

Deakin, F. W. *The Brutal Friendship*, Weidenfeld and Nicolson, London, 1962

Giamberaderi, Admiral di *La Marina nella Tragedia Nazionale*, Donesi, Rome, 1960

Edmonds, J. E. *A History of World War I*, Longmans, London, 1965

Esposito, General V. J. *A Concise History of World War One*, Pall Mall, London, 1970

Faldella, F. *L'Italia e la Seconda Guerra Mondiale*, Cappelli, Rome,

Farnie, D. A. *East and West of Suez*, O.U.P., London, 1968

Flaccomio, S. *Obbedire e Combattere*, Longanesi, Milan, 1970

Fraccaruli, A. *Italian Warships of World War One*, Ian Allan, London, 1970

Giglio, V. and Ravenni, A. *Le Guerre Coloniale d'Italia*, Casa Editrice, Milan, 1935

Gilbert, M. *The European Powers, 1900–1945*, Plume, London, 1970

Gottlieb, W. W. *Studies in Secret Diplomacy during the First World War*, Allen and Unwin, London, 1957

Grant, J. *Cassell's History of the War in the Soudan*, Cassell, London, 1887
Grasselli, Colonel E. *L'Esercito Italiano in Francia e in Oriente*, Corbaccio, Milan, 1957
Grebler, L. and Winkler, W. *The Cost of the World War to Germany and to Austria-Hungary*, Yale U.P., New Haven, 1940
Guarglia, R. *Ricordi*, Librarie Plon, Paris, 1955
Holt, P. M. *The Mahdist State in the Sudan, 1881–1898*, O.U.P., London, 1958
Hoptner, J. B. *Yugoslavia in Crisis, 1934–1941*, Columbia U.P., New York, 1963
Hubatsch, W. *Germany and the Central Powers in the World War, 1914–1918*, University of Kansas, Lawrence, 1963
Kindelan, General A. *La Guerra en el Mediterraneo y el Norte de Africa*, Idea, Madrid, 1965
Lafore, L. *The Long Fuse*, Lippincott, New York, 1966
Lapworth, C. *Tripoli and Young Italy*, Swift, London, 1912
Laurens, F. Y. *Frame and the Italo-Ethiopian Crisis, 1935–1936*, Mouton, The Hague, 1967
Lazzati, G. *I Soliti Quattro Galli*, Marsia, Milan, 1965
Lederer, I. J. *Yugoslavia at the Paris Peace Conference*, Yale U.P., New Haven, 1963
Macartney, C. A. *October Fifteenth: A History of Modern Hungary, 1929–1945*, Edinburgh U.P., 1968
MacIntyre, D. *The Battle for the Mediterranean*, Pan, London, 1966
May, A. J. *The Habsburg Monarchy, 1867–1914*, Harvard U.P., Cambridge, 1951
Missiroli, M. *Ce Que l'Italie Doit a Mussolini*, Edizione di Novissima, Rome, 1938
Mondini, L. *Prologo del Conflitto Italo-Greco*, Treves, Rome, 1945
Moorhead, A. *The White Nile*, Hamilton, London, 1961
Naval Intelligence Division, *Yugoslavia*, H.M.S.O., Norwich, 1945
Paglioni, F. *Aviatori Italiani*, Longanesi, Milan, 1970
Pignatelli, L. *La Guerra dei Seite Mesi*, Editorial Mezzogiorno, Naples, 1940
Potter, F. B. and Nimitz, C. W. *Sea Power*, Prentice-Hall, New Jersey, 1961
Royal Institute of International Affairs, *Survey of International Affairs*, 1920–1923, 1925, 1934, 1935, 1936, O.U.P., London
Salandra, A. *Italy and the Great War*, Arnold, London, 1932
Salvatorelli, L. and Mira, G. *Storia d'Italia Nel Periodo Fascista*, Einaudi, Turin, 1964
Salvemini, G. *Prelude to World War II*, Gollancz, London, 1953
Santoro, General G. *L'Aeronautica Italiana nella IIa Guerra Mondiale*, Donesi, Rome, 1950
Seton-Watson, C. *Italy from Liberalism to Fascism, 1870–1925*, Methuen, London, 1967
Seton-Watson, R. W. *Europe in the Melting-Pot*, Macmillan, London, 1919
Shankland, P. and Hunter, A. *Malta Convoy*, Fontana, London, 1969
Smith, P. *Pedestal*, Kimber, London, 1971

Stafford, F. *The Far and the Deep*, Barker, London, 1968
Stamp, Sir Josiah *Studies in Current Problems in Finance and Government*, King, London, 1924
Stavrianos, L. *The Balkans Since 1453*, Winston, New York, 1965
Taylor, A. J. P. *The Struggle for Mastery in Europe, 1848–1918*, O.U.P., London, 1957
Taylor, John W. R. *Combat Aircraft of the World*, Michael Joseph, London, 1970
Thomas, H. *The Spanish Civil War*, Pelican, London, 1968
The Times History of the South African War, London, 1912
Valori, F. *Gli Italiani in Russia*, Bieli, Milan, 1967
Villari, L. *The Expansion of Italy*, Faber and Faber, London, 1930
Williams, A. *Air Power*, Macmillan, New York, 1937
Wiskemann, E. *Europe of the Dictators*, Fontana, London, 1966
Wiskemann, E. *The Rome-Berlin Axis*, Fontana, London, 1966
Woytinsky, W. S. and E. S. *World Commerce and Governments*, The Twentieth Century Fund, New York, 1955

Index